Praise for *The Fina Guide to Investing in Funds*

'This book highlights the many pitfalls that investors often overlook or do not understand when investing. This includes a range of investment vehicles ranging from offshore hedge funds through to onshore regulated vehicles. Far too often, investors place too much reliance on brand names or regulators to protect themselves or to defend an investment decision. Jérôme Lussan has been able to provide thought provoking insight, especially with respect to operational investment issues. A must-have tool in your investment kit!'

Marc de Kloe, *Senior Product Specialist, Head of Hedge Funds,*
ABN AMRO Private Banking

'This book is a timely and valuable guide for fund investors. I very much enjoyed reading it. By building on his practical experience and a range of excellent case studies Jérôme Lussan successfully highlights the importance of taking a comprehensive approach to fund evaluation in order to make successful investments.'

Professor Robert Kosowski, *Director of Risk Management Lab and*
Centre for Hedge Fund Research, Imperial College London

'With his deep knowledge of the industry and his pragmatic approach, Lussan gives not only an exhaustive overview of the organization, structure and service providers involved in investment funds but he also covers comprehensively actual developments in the industry, such as risk management or compliance and offers to the reader some insightful case studies. Accessible and understandable but at the same time thorough and critical.'

Paolo Vinciarelli, *Head of Investment Funds, BCEE Luxembourg*

'Investors are invariably seduced by return patterns. They might do better and follow the Bard's advice to 'Let every eye negotiate for itself and trust no agent.' This helpful book suggests the best ways investors might improve their eye for better managed funds and hopefully better returns.'

Edmund Bellord, *Asset Allocation Portfolio Strategist, GMO LLC*

'Hedge fund investing requires a blend of art and science which Lussan understands well and this comes out from the book, and provides an invaluable insight from a leading expert. *The Financial Times Guide to Investing in Funds* teaches readers how to be disciplined when investing to obtain the right disclosures to ensure the protection of their assets. Read this book and you will learn how due diligence principles can protect your investments.'

Nathanael Benzaken, *Managing Director, Head of Managed Account Development, Lyxor Asset Management*

'This is a comprehensive guide for all professionals and investors into the due diligence process behind picking the right fund for their portfolio. Too many investors focus simply on fund statistics and the manager's underlying strategy and neglect the basics of good fund management which includes corporate governance, regulatory controls and elementary accounting. This impressive new book makes amends and forces the investor to think about the actual structure of fund management and understand how it can so easily go wrong – along the way Lussan fleshes out his analysis with real world examples of investment disasters including the notorious Bernard Madoff affair. An essential read for any sophisticated investor.'

David Stevenson, *Financial Times Adventurous Investor Columnist*

The Financial Times Guide to Investing in Funds

How to select investments, assess managers and protect your wealth

Jérôme de Lavenère Lussan

Harlow, England • London • New York • Boston • San Francisco • Toronto • Sydney • Auckland • Singapore • Hong Kong
Tokyo • Seoul • Taipei • New Delhi • Cape Town • São Paulo • Mexico City • Madrid • Amsterdam • Munich • Paris • Milan

PEARSON EDUCATION LIMITED

Edinburgh Gate
Harlow CM20 2JE
Tel: +44 (0)1279 623623
Fax: +44 (0)1279 431059
Website: www.pearson.com/uk

First published in Great Britain in 2012

© Pearson Education Limited 2012

The right of Jérôme de Lavenère Lussan to be identified as author of this work has been asserted by him in accordance with the Copyright, Designs and Patents Act 1988.

Pearson Education is not responsible for the content of third-party internet sites.

ISBN: 978-0-273-73285-3

British Library Cataloguing-in-Publication Data
A catalogue record for this book is available from the British Library

Library of Congress Cataloging-in-Publication Data
Lavenère Lussan, Jérôme de.
 The Financial times guide to investing in funds : how to select investments, assess managers and protect your wealth / Jérôme de Lavenère Lussan.
   p. cm.
 Includes bibliographical references and index.
 ISBN 978-0-273-73285-3 (pbk.)
 1. Mutual funds. 2. Investments. I. Title. II. Title: Investing in funds.
 HG4530.L356 2012
 332.63'27--dc23
                              2012011365

The Financial Times. With a worldwide network of highly respected journalists, The Financial Times provides global business news, insightful opinion and expert analysis of business, finance and politics. With over 500 journalists reporting from 50 countries worldwide, our in-depth coverage of international news is objectively reported and analysed from an independent, global perspective. To find out more, visit www.ft.com/pearsonoffer.

10 9 8 7 6 5 4 3 2 1
15 14 13 12

Typeset in 9pt Stone Serif by 30
Printed and bound in Great Britain by Ashford Colour Press Ltd, Gosport, Hampshire

Contents

Acknowledgements

I would like to thank my wife Sophie. I thank her for pushing me to do this book and write regularly. I truly benefitted from her encouragement and she created enough time for me to write the book whilst having two children. I also thank my team at Laven Partners and Laven Legal for their help. Miranda Dewdney-Herbert and Oliver Quarmby helped with the initial logistics which helped to launch the project. Sara Magrath, Tanja Salonen, Indre Dargyte, Max Ferri, Alexandra Tzalla and Petra Hollis provided research and insights along the way helping me complete each chapter with the appropriate sources and details. Finally I want to thank David Stevenson for giving me the idea to take on the project of writing the book, starting in May 2009, and Chris Cudmore for having the patience to review and publish it.

Publisher's acknowledgements

We are grateful to the following for permission to reproduce copyright material:

The Financial Times for permission to reproduce 'Pension funds fear EU hedge funds rules' by Martin Arnold, 13 January 2010.

In some instances we have been unable to trace the owners of copyright material and would appreciate any information that would enable us to do so.

Introduction

This book will teach you how to select funds based on the reliability of their business models and investment strategies. It will teach you how to understand the details of investment processes used by asset managers as well as the quality and substance of their operations. In addition you will learn about investment advisors and other service providers that are in the business of recommending funds or servicing funds. After reading this book you will be able to understand, like never before, how funds operate and the obvious, and not so obvious, pitfalls everyone should avoid. I will explain, in simple practical terms, what all investors should know. The ideas and explanations in this book are comprehensive but simple. They can be used by sophisticated professionals as well as regular private investors with an interest in challenging the accepted wisdom of their advisors. I will also point you to many websites and other resources to help you investigate funds and asset managers quickly and cheaply, if not for free.

Of course, any author with the ambition of explaining things in simple terms is confronted with the hard reality that there are many technical terms used in the fund management industry. To help I have included my own, non-technical, glossary. You can refer to it whenever you see a defined word, which will be emphasised in bold in the text when it is first used in each chapter.

My real introduction to the investment fund industry came in 2003 when I was asked to join a leading hedge fund, Rhicon Currency Management, by an old university friend and star trader, Christopher Brandon. Prior to that, I had worked as a solicitor on international financial transactions and fund structures in the City of London at Jones Day. My understanding of funds, other than their legal structure, was limited. When I was exposed to the funds world, and specifically to the hedge fund world, I felt like I had been dropped in the middle of the Channel, in the cold of winter, and asked to make my way back to the white cliffs of Dover pretty much on my own! I loved it, and I quickly realised that funds were very ordinary structures, ultimately controlled by asset managers situated in major financial centres like New York, London or Paris. Knowing that, it struck me that this was not how they were sold to investors, the focus being placed on the fund itself, sometimes a pooling vehicle established in some remote country.

From my private equity expertise of buying and selling companies for clients, it dawned on me that investors should consider funds by reviewing the asset manager's business, just as they would buying into any other business. I wanted to explain to investors that asset managers had many attributes and weaknesses and that this was the most relevant information that investors needed to consider, not the track record, nor even the legal establishment of the fund in isolation. It is the asset manager's team and its operations that matter most with regards to the sustainable life and performance of the fund. The genius of some asset managers is only one aspect of that and, in the wrong business context, they will struggle to succeed, however much they are geniuses. From that premise, I endeavoured to coach investors to understand how that business works. I felt that this process of education was the strongest safeguard against choosing the wrong fund. I think anyone can achieve this understanding.

In this book I aggregate all of my coaching efforts and hope to give, for the first time, a new and complete picture of the business of asset managers and the funds they run. Where possible I use hard facts and case studies to illustrate many points, usually involving hedge funds as they tend to be more liberal and therefore at times more likely to pose a risk. Bear in mind that hedge funds can be lurking in any portfolio (now as UCITS too), so even if you do not contemplate direct investments in hedge funds, you may well be exposed to them through structured products or funds of funds sold to you by your bank.

I decided to write this book in May 2009, largely as a result of the impact of the financial crisis on investors. I felt that investors had been hard done by the industry. Those exposed to long only funds found that there was little diversification in their portfolios. Those exposed to hedge funds were in some cases even worse off: having believed that they had been sold some protection, they still found that most of their money was in correlated losing strategies. It was worse for those who were exposed to frauds, like Madoff and Weavering Capital. In some cases, if it was not fraud it was complete negligence and operational failures at the fund and manager level, which left investors with huge losses. What made it worse was that the financial crisis exposed the unbelievable abuse by some financial professionals of their trusting investor clients. This tore through the age old relationship of trust that used to exist between banker and client underpinned by the famous London Stock Exchange motto 'my word is my bond'. It remains very fragile to this day as standards, notably in risk management, have to improve. I want to improve the industry, as we all badly need it to do well if we want to survive on our pensions. I believe this is possible if we can strengthen the knowledge around funds, knowledge which at present is inadequate and often skewed by an over-simplistic non-specialised media.

In fact, since 2008, the media's dislike of asset managers, reflected in popular opinion, has been very visible … funds, funds of funds, funds of hedge funds and hedge funds are all referred to regularly with regards to losses or frauds. This one-sided view is inevitably biased. There are many things to be explained but funds and alternative funds in particular actually do protect investors. Our pensions would be well served by using alternative strategies such as those offered by hedge funds. The standard of what is on offer, however, has to be improved and explanations have to be given as to why some funds did so remarkably badly and why some financial advisors, including private bankers, basically misled, deliberately or not, investors. This is, in part, what this book will aim to do. I also hope to give enough material for you to make up your mind as to what kind of fund you want to invest into. In essence, I aim to give you enough information to make a difference.

I trust that after reading this book you will continue to invest in all types of funds, including hedge funds, in an intelligent and beneficial way. I am very much in favour of even the most complicated funds, if you understand clearly what they do, as good asset managers will provide more stable returns over the long term. It is not easy to select funds, but with this book in hand you will have a much better chance of success. Former chairman of the FSA, Callum McCarthy, stated in July 2007 that the regulator was open to hedge funds expanding into the retail market as long as 'investors are properly informed about the risks and opportunities of these products'. This book is part of the information that I think the industry should be making freely available. I have not seen much of it being disseminated since Mr McCarthy's call and perhaps this book will encourage funds and financial professionals to open up about their businesses.

I had two aims when I started writing this book. First I wanted to provide a self-help method, for all types of investors, but notably those already involved in fund selection, to appreciate what was being done with their money so that they could avoid being tempted by the sales pitches and focus on the facts. This book is therefore aimed at empowering investors in their own right. By doing so I hope that it will lead to improvements in the asset management industry.

Second, I decided to write this book for the regular investor, not necessarily an expert but one who works through advisors, and who was disappointed in 2008, feeling let down and not well advised. Of the many people who provide advisory and research services on funds, few are willing to share how they go about doing this or are prepared to educate investors with actual details of how to review the operations as well as investment processes of asset managers. Usually it is because those who provide such services tend to make their living off of their work, quite naturally, and so would rather sell this information through the provision of services. The same applies to financial advisors and funds of funds. It is what they perceive as their unique selling point or their competitive advantage. What is regretable is that even investors who buy the services do not get access to the actual research and therefore still rely on service providers making promises as to their own skills and processes but with no guarantees. It is very easy for professionals to hide behind the usual jargon of the industry; and hard on investors who only discover after the event their advisors' failings. What is worse is that, as we saw after 2008, there is very little investors can do after a crisis to recoup their losses as contractually advisors and asset managers are usually very well protected.

I think it is imperative for investors to know how their current and future service providers, be they private banks, independent financial advisors and so on, operate; to know what reliance they can place on those selling their services to them as experts. I also believe that any service provider who does not want to fully open up their investment or research process is to be treated with a certain scepticism. I do not believe that their research should be viewed like the secret formula of Coca-Cola. The success of fund selection and financial research and analysis is not about secret processes; it is about hard work, hours of it, combined with skills and expertise covering many areas of specialism relevant to the fund industry. Research and advisory services in this respect are relatively easy to assess, once you are organised and have the know-how. It just takes a lot of time and regular updating, as structures and financial instruments change and evolve. The bulk of your work should be to verify information, to spot the exaggerations (and sometimes lies) that some asset managers are happy to present without scruples. I can prove that over the years you cannot cheat a skilful verification process.

In this book I will give you my tips and those from my team's direct experience that will help you avoid bad investment decisions – as we say at Laven 'Trust but verify!' It may not save you time, but it will save you money.

That is my secret and I am happy to share it!

1

The manager

What topics are covered in this chapter?

- The star traders
- International legal structures for managers
- The manager and the advisor's roles
- Controls over the fund
- What to deduce from a manager's set up

When you read or hear about **funds** you usually think of the 'fund', not the other companies that work for the fund. Yet it is those companies that make the fund a reality. It is also often assumed that the fund is in the UK or the US, or when you read about funds that make the headlines it is implied that they are near you and not miles away in a foreign jurisdiction. This is particularly true for hedge funds. For instance, the other day I read an article in the *Sunday Times* which mistakenly referred to 'London hedge funds'. Hedge funds are in fact not in the UK but **offshore**. It is the investment management company of the fund that is in the UK. It is again the investment management company that everyone, from the press to the politicians, refers to when talking about funds. This is the company that is of interest to you, and you should be carefully studying it if you want to ensure that the fund you are investing into will deliver according to its promises.

Most investors still focus too much of their attention on the fund, as opposed to the investment management company, prior to making an investment decision; therefore they are at risk of not understanding what is actually happening to their money. It makes sense, of course, to look at the fund, notably for two reasons: it has the money, and it is the company that performs well or loses. It is however a simple and naive approach to simply limit your scrutiny to the fund, which could be characterised as just a shell, and is indeed subject to manipulation by the investment management company which has ultimate control. This form of control and potential for abuse was exemplified by the Madoff fraud (discussed in detail later), one which investors would have been able to spot had they invested their time to review the operations of the investment management company.

I have always believed that you cannot start to understand a fund without a solid appreciation of the investment management team and its organisation as a business. It is this company, the **manager** as it is commonly known and a term that I will use in this book, that is most relevant to what will happen to your money. I think that there are more reasons to look at the manager and its processes than to look at the fund that it manages. You can review information on the manager's investment processes, corporate governance, organisational structure and overall risk management to really understand how it actually manages the money you placed in the fund. This is the *raison d'être* of the manager and the fund cannot function without it.

Another reason for this focus is that although we all know that past performance is not indicative of future results, performance is more likely to last if the management team is reliable and well organised. A fund will only function if the manager's staff and principals act in accordance with what is in the fund's and thus the investors' best interests. The manager itself, as a corporate entity, has the responsibility for investing the money which you as an investor put into a fund.

In this chapter, I will explain how the manager functions, including how it invests your money; and how you can seek to control what is being done as your money flows from one company to another under the manager's control. I will look at what causes money to go from one bank to another, or how your money is used to achieve leverage when the fund uses it to borrow more money. I will also, therefore, tell you how to work out how your money can end up invested in securities or shares that might not have been part of the original investment strategy when you chose to invest in the fund.

The star traders

To understand managers you have to understand their leaders, those behind the set up of the funds, because they are or believe themselves to be star traders. They are commonly referred to in the industry as the 'principals' or the 'partners'. They are usually traders who have gathered with one or two people to establish the manager. In the US most managers are organised as limited liability corporations, thus the sobriquet of 'principal'. In the UK they can be organised as limited liability partnerships, thus the use of 'partners'. They are easy to identify from their reputation or indeed from the documentation provided to investors by managers. The first document usually made available is the fund's marketing presentation, which includes a description of the main members of the manager's team. This will, in practice, include a summarised biography of each member.

I always think it is good to review these biographies, as this is a quick and indicative indication of the general background of those involved. At least ensure that the background, notably market experience for traders and other knowledge for operations managers, matches what you are being told. Of course, just as any CV can be embellished, the same is true of those biographies and trust me sometimes they are! So I tend to remain cautious and always verify the information. If you have the opportunity, carry out more complex **background checks**. I give you more information on how to do that in Chapter 10. This is useful as any check that does not bring out the information you expect should put you on alert.

International legal structures for managers

Managers are usually organised in the way depicted below. The funds in themselves tend to be simple legal structures: however, legal complexity arises from the relationships that the fund has with the manager and other companies (including custodians, brokerage firms and **administrators**) that provide services to it. For the purpose of this chapter, I focus on the most common international structures of funds and managers. Note that in these international structures the manager may also be assisted by an **advisor**, another entity that might end up being the one that controls your assets. I explain that relationship in further detail below.

Look at the first diagram in Figure 1.1. The fund is usually a company incorporated in a jurisdiction where it does not suffer any taxation on profits. The fund will almost always delegate its responsibilities to service providers and will notably delegate the management of the investment strategy to the chosen manager which, as we saw, is a separate corporate entity specialising in asset management. This is reflected in a contract called an **investment management agreement** and this

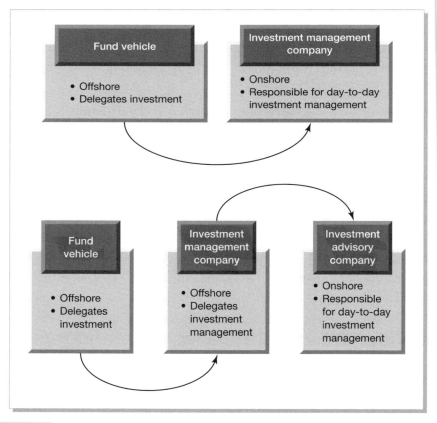

Figure 1.1   The fund relationships

is the official contractual link between the fund and the manager. The manager can in turn sub-delegate, as shown in the second diagram in Figure 1.1, some or all of its powers to one or more sub-manager(s) or to an advisor. In some cases, this delegation is truly at arm's length but in other cases the companies are founded and controlled by the same individuals, and structured in this way for commercial and tax reasons. This relationship is governed by an **investment advisory agreement**.

If you grasp the business structure in detail then you will develop a stronger understanding of the controls that affect risks and investment processes. Ultimately this translates into knowing who, of the people you read about in the fund's literature, does what and where. To get your head around this is reassuring because, at the end of the day, you want to identify who really has the power to play with your money, and unfortunately there are no explicit disclosure rules that exist about this.

The manager and the advisor's roles

To take the points above further, when you invest in funds you are putting your money into the hands of what you believe is a talented investment team in the hope of making a return thanks to their investment expertise. In reality, you make an investment into a fund with its own **board of directors** and corporate life. It is very likely, as we saw, that for alternative funds, the fund is not even in the UK. It is often domiciled on an island where there is no tax so as to maximise the benefits for investors. The fund is managed by an **onshore** manager, subject to a contract that you should ask to see. This manager is usually located in cities like London or New York.

Sometimes there is another layer added if the manager is also offshore. In that case the offshore manager delegates advisory and/or managerial services to what is called an advisor or sub-manager. This company is again in a major financial services centre, notably London or New York. It is usually called the 'advisor' and I shall refer to it as such in this book. It has the same characteristics as the manager and for the purposes of this book what applies to one generally applies to the other. I want you to appreciate its purpose because it is very easy to get confused, and an appreciation of the overall structure will strengthen your understanding of who does what with your money.

For clarity and simplicity in this book my focus is on the manager. Where you come across references to an advisor, you have to give careful attention to a second company. You can take all of the points I make about the manager and use them to make a similar analysis of the advisor. The fund itself, as we shall see in Chapter 2, does not actually do much. The use of all these companies, which are often related, raises a concern regarding conflicts of interest. You need to get comfortable with that.

Conflicts of interest

One of the problems with the industry is that it is full of potential conflicts of interest. Where you would think that independent companies should be providing checks and balances you find that there are common interests and influences that limit or do away with any independence. So be aware of this and be prepared to dig further. To understand how conflicts of interest are controlled and to avoid confusion, when you meet a manager, an advisor or its representatives, it is vital that you ask them about the degree of independence that exists between each of the relevant contractual parties. If this is not clear, you may find out that your money is actually placed in the care of a company far from home and which itself may be managed by related persons but not subject to proper checks.

You should therefore seek clarity regarding relationships between any of the individuals or companies you read about in the fund's documentation. This is very important information and you must look for connections that appear suspiciously cosy if you want to avoid a Madoff or Weavering Capital fraud (covered in detail in this chapter and in Chapter 4 respectively). One of the main reasons for fraud or operational failures occurring is existing conflicts of interest, which, at some point in time are abused. An obvious example of a big warning sign is when a manager works with a related or affiliated brokerage firm. Madoff is a perfect illustration but it is not an isolated case and even banks – small and large – that run their own funds will suffer from similar conflicts.

Madoff's Ponzi scheme

In brief:

▨ The case involved a fraudulent $65 billion investment empire

▨ Bernie Madoff founded Bernard L. Madoff Investment Securities LLC (BMIS) in 1960 and was the company's chairman until end 2008

▨ BMIS managed multiple feeder funds worth approximately $65 billion

▨ BMIS was one of the top investment firms on Wall Street, but instead of investing clients' money in securities, money was held with a related depositor; new deposits were used to pay out redemptions, whilst false returns were portrayed to investors

▨ In late 2008 Madoff admitted to defrauding thousands of investors of $65 billion

▨ In June 2009 Madoff was sentenced to 150 years in prison

Madoff, founder and chairman of Bernard L. Madoff Investment Securities LLC (BMIS) was arrested in December 2008 for masterminding and operating the largest 'Ponzi' scheme in history, which defrauded thousands of investors of billions of dollars. Essentially, instead of placing investors' money in securities, the money was held with his related brokerage company and new deposits were used to pay redemptions, whilst in the meantime false performance results were given to investors, helping to maintain the impression that the business was successful.

Madoff was a former American investment advisor, stockbroker and non-executive chairman of NASDAQ, giving him very strong credentials. In 1960, Madoff founded the Wall Street firm BMIS. The firm was one of the most successful businesses on Wall Street until late 2008 when Madoff allegedly confessed to his sons that the asset management arm of BMIS, in which he claimed to manage $65 billion of investors' money, was a 'big lie'. His sons consequently informed authorities of their father's confession and Madoff was arrested the following day. Madoff insisted, to everyone's amazement, that he was solely responsible for the fraud. In March 2009, he pleaded guilty to 11 federal crimes which included securities fraud, wire fraud, mail fraud, money laundering, making false statements and false filings with the US Securities and Exchange Commission (SEC), the US watchdog. In June 2009, he was given a 150-year prison sentence.

▶

Federal investigators believe that the fraud may have begun as early as the 1980s. The size and scope of the Ponzi scheme attracted much media attention, especially given the fact that the company's history of failing to comply with regulatory enforcements, previous lawsuits and fines should have signalled issues to investors and USA regulatory authorities. For instance, concerns about Madoff's business arose as early as 1999, when a financial analyst informed the SEC that BMIS's gains were legally and mathematically impossible to achieve. Prior to 2008, BMIS was subject to investigations by both the SEC and the NASD, yet neither saw its internal failures.

A lawsuit in December 1994 should also have highlighted warning signals to investors: BMIS was a defendant in a lawsuit initiated by Datek Securities Corporation regarding an 'alleged bias and conflict of interest'. In addition, BMIS received a total of $66,000 in NASD fines between 1963 and 2008, which although not unusual, should have, in context, added to the warning signs. Despite all of this, BMIS was one of the top Wall Street firms. Madoff's success presumably lay in the fact that he ran his business like an exclusive club and would throw out investors who asked too many questions. Most investors had invested in BMIS through personal recommendation, and were willingly ignorant of the risks and bad regulatory history associated with it.

Some of the most obvious warning signs should have come from the conflicts that existed in the structure. The legal framework meant that BMIS was responsible for many accounts including fund accounts set up by UBS and HSBC in Europe and Switzerland. BMIS was the ultimate depositor of assets, which in itself is seen as giving rise to conflicts of interest. Had investors been able to appreciate the facts of the legal framework, they would have acted more cautiously. It is therefore important to understand who you are working with. If you buy a Coke from Coca-Cola it is not the same thing as buying cola from a fake manufacturer purporting to be Coca-Cola. With Madoff you were sold the UBS brand with no health warnings that the product had very little to do with UBS!

In the end Madoff was caught because the crisis of 2008, which caused a lot of investors to lose money, meant that they all went to Madoff to get money that they believed to be safe and which in fact had benefited from gains. Without this it is likely the story would have gone on and the losses been even worse, however unbelievable that may seem now.

Lessons learned

1 Understand the type of investment strategy the manager uses.

- The 'split strike conversion' strategy raised a lot of concerns in that it was near impossible for it to deliver the types of returns announced by BMIS.

- BMIS had an unusual pattern of returns which did not align to any strategy or at least not the type of strategy purported to be used in relevant documentation/**prospectuses**.

- The strategy showed advantageous lack of correlation to any other type of strategy, which was unusual in the context of normal investment results even for the most talented of managers.

2 Consider the appropriateness of commission charges.

- Why would BMIS only charge commissions (which represented less than 0.50 per cent of AUM) for the management of the feeder funds when it could have charged 2–20 per cent as was the norm in the industry? This apparent good deal and generosity was probably designed to allow resellers to charge most of the fees that investors ended up paying and thus led more intermediaries to introduce more of their client base. This reflects the importance of understanding who is being paid by whom. There is strong evidence that the conflicts of interest created by Madoff's approach were the cause of his 'success'.

3 Pay attention to controls by family members.

- In focusing on the company that has control over your money you need to appreciate who are the individuals and what their expertise is, or if there could be any natural conflicts that would affect their actions. In Madoff's case there was a heavy reliance on family members taking key positions in BMIS. For example:

  - brother, Peter Madoff, Senior Managing Director, Head of Trading, and Chief Compliance Officer;

  - son, Mark Madoff, Director of Listed Trading;

  - son, Andrew Madoff, Director of NASDAQ Trading;

  - nephew, Charles Weiner, Director of Administration;

  - niece, Shana Madoff, Compliance Officer.

▶

---

4 Take a look into the past history of the company.

  ▨ Madoff's history of numerous investigations, a lawsuit and regulatory fines should have been a warning to investors.

  ▨ The structure of the Madoff companies would also have been identifiable by the results of regulators' reports and a review of the relevant regulators' publicly available information.

5 Perform background checks on key individuals.

  ▨ Background checks would have revealed certain weaker qualities of some of the BMIS staff. For example, Frank DiPascali, Jr., the CFO and Director of Trading, was a college dropout, had no previous work experience, and had a history of unpaid taxes and late filing of taxes.

As an investor you should remain vigilant and where possible ask about conflicts of interest that you may have picked up. Ask whether there are internal checks and audits to protect from such conflicts. In some jurisdictions the local regulator of the manager may require that it publishes or provides clients with a conflict of interest policy and you could ask to see that too. Remember that you need to ask for such information as it is not usually volunteered by managers. In fact, the FSA, and by the same token other EU regulators, aware of existing conflicts between service providers and managers, have strict rules about, for example, accepting or paying fees or other benefits to or from service providers. This includes soft commission (dealing commissions), which are forbidden except under certain limited conditions. Managers must make disclosures about any such fees if they are paid or accepted. This information will not usually form part of the documentation you may be given, but it must exist, so I find that it is worth asking for.

Unfortunately many investors accept that it is hard for them to request or obtain information let alone read and digest it. There is also a feeling of powerlessness as you cannot really change much if conflicts of interest are prominent even if you can always walk away. In reality, as you will know from reading the financial press, it is not uncommon for some abuse to take place, for example in relation to dealing commissions, even between non-connected managers and brokerage firms. There were also many instances of insider trading or market abuse reported in 2010 and 2011. If the authorities really start to put more resources into investigations then more cases can be expected in the years to come.

So should you do nothing? I don't think so and there is a lot that can be found out from the simple information I suggest you obtain. For example it will tell you that any risk of conflicts of interest has been identified and minimised by the manager. That it takes the issue seriously (or not) and that therefore the business is likely to be better run as a result. You can also take the documents provided by the fund's marketing team, notably the marketing presentation and the prospectus, and just check which companies are named as servicing the fund or manager. If they look connected you should be worried and ask more questions about their independence.

It is also clear that where a manager might control the **broker** (the company that takes market orders for the relevant fund), there is room for concern and you must ensure that proper procedures are in place to avoid any conflicts of interest. Likewise such conflicts are made worse if the manager also has responsibility for the custody of your cash.

Fly-by-night attitude to contracts

Many investors remain unaware of the contracts that their fund has with service providers. This is a big problem, as today's world of unread contracts means that they can contain just about anything that can prejudice investors – as seen in the case of Madoff. Indeed one of the aspects of the industry that is often misunderstood, and which I elaborate upon in Chapter 7, is that the fund is never represented legally in a way that protects investors. The fund is just a legal envelope into which investors deposit their money, and it is the brain-child of a manager. It is the manager that appoints lawyers who will then act for the fund. What they recommend in any contract may easily conflict with what may be in the interest of investors. Investors are of course not present when the lawyers are appointed and even if they are shareholders of the fund they have no influence on the type of contracts the fund will have, including the prospectus. I think that in the future investors who are better prepared, willing to read contracts and who understand these legal issues will have a better chance of avoiding such pitfalls.

By way of contrast, in a private equity deal, all the contracts of the company are carefully studied for any liabilities they may contain, and any investment of money which is also the subject of a subscription, much like in a fund, is carefully negotiated. When you invest in a fund this never appears to be the case!

Controls over the fund

There is a final dimension to the legal structure. As any normal company, the fund and any manager/advisor it may delegate to are owned by shareholders who have the potential to vote and therefore to wield significant influence over the companies' behaviour. The shareholders are referred to in the regulatory world as **controllers**, whether they are individuals or companies, and whether they actually have ownership or potentially have the power to influence management. Typically the board of directors of the fund will also be made up of individuals from the manager or the advisor. The controllers are relevant as they can have a significant impact on the actions of the fund or the manager/advisor and may also be subject to conflicts of interest, for example, where the ownership of the fund is in the same hands as that of the manager. In fact, think about this for a moment. Although very common, you can see an immediate conflict in that the board of the fund may no longer independently determine whether the actions of the manager, with which it has a connection, are being taken for the benefit of the fund's investors. This could include a fund deciding to prevent the redemption of your investment, sometimes for reasons that might hardly be credible, as was the case in 2009.

A good example of when preventing the exit of investors may not be in the best interest of investors is when an investment strategy has failed to deliver returns or has incurred some significant losses, but not crashed and burned. Imagine you are invested in such a strategy. The manager may still wish to continue to get paid a management fee in order to sustain its business and therefore keep your money in the fund. You on the other hand would rather have your money back as you may simply need the cash or prefer to invest in another opportunity. During the financial crisis of 2008, this led to the obvious question for some boards of directors of funds: what should they do? The choice was to suspend redemptions or to raise **gates** to delay the process of redemption, or indeed to give money back to investors. This had to be decided by funds largely at the bequest of the manager that had a direct interest in continuing to be paid as opposed to progressing on the basis of what was in the best interest of investors. Today this remains controversial: even as I write, many of the gates that were raised after 2008 remain in place. What made things worse was that you, as an investor, would have had no say in the matter, particularly in relation to any offshore fund as most of these have non-voting share classes for investors.

Now, it is not always in the best interest of investors to release their money, as sometimes the resulting need to sell the fund's assets quickly reduces the overall value that can be given back to other investors. Many board members of funds still feel victimised by the stigma that followed 2008 regarding their lack of independence. In some cases of course this is justified. The suspension of redemptions can give a manager more time to realise the potential value on the sale of the assets held by the fund, especially if the assets are illiquid and there is no market for them at that time. This may in certain circumstances be better than a quick fire sale. Nonetheless I have seen more cases of complaints than of total satisfaction. I think it is a matter of balance of powers and at present the balance is heavily tipped in favour of those who control the fund and its board.

Legally this is what a board of directors and an investor will have to work from. A typical clause allowing a fund to potentially suspend redemptions (meaning stopping all pending and future redemptions) could be as follows:

> The managers may suspend redemptions of shares during any period in which: any circumstances exist as a result of which it is not reasonably practicable for the company to dispose of significant assets or instruments owned by it or as a result of which any such disposal would be detrimental to shareholders; and any such suspension shall take effect at such time as the manager shall declare and shall continue until the manager shall declare such suspension at an end.

As you can see, the power given to the manager in this clause is very broad and it would not be too difficult for managers to justify to the fund's board of directors that suspending the fund's redemptions and keeping them suspended for an undetermined period of time is right. Meanwhile the shareholders are locked in.

During the 2008 financial crisis, managers used these suspension rights without much notable regard for the best interest of investors. Most shareholders in offshore funds had no voting rights and therefore had no right of consultation to determine with the managers what was in their best interest. What is clear is that in some cases these powers, combined with either weak corporate governance or bad management of conflicts of interest, did not lead to fair decisions on behalf of the fund's investors.

Another aspect of control seems to have been lost in the use of feeder funds. Feeder funds simply invest all of their assets into another fund. So the service providers of the actual fund are in effect substituted for those of the feeder fund. This may not always be explicit and you need to be careful about this as it creates a whole new layer of risk since you may not know who has control of the fund that ends up having your money.

What is regrettable is that the structures of controls have not been improved since the financial crisis, so it's important that you understand who controls all the companies that work for the fund and who controls the fund indirectly.

Feeder funds – why they confused investors in the Madoff case

If you think about it, Madoff was a grand scale fraud, hidden, in some cases, behind a layer of feeder funds that had all the characteristics of legitimate products. They were fronted by the right financial institutions but in the end those institutions appear to have had pretty much no legal responsibility for the products offered. This shows that the delegation aspect of any fund structure is important since in the end the only person that takes responsibility for your money appears to be you …

What's a feeder fund? A feeder fund is a fund, in that it has a legal format that allows investors to participate just like any other fund. It also signs up the usual service providers, including custodian and administrator, and the lawyers and **auditors** too. It has its own board if it is incorporated as a company. The fund's main characteristic, which defines it as a feeder, is that it will only invest its money into another fund. It is a pure conduit (thus the word 'feeder'), sending the money it has received to another fund. This other fund will have its own custodian and administrator again as well as its other service providers.

Why did Madoff use feeder funds? He concentrated his management business so that it was all done in-house, including administration and custody. This therefore meant that his company or related companies, including a small firm of auditors over which he is believed to have had substantial influence would do the work of looking after the assets his companies would receive. Since there was a regulated securities company acting as depositor and a legally separate, albeit related, manager, the use of feeder funds was perfectly logical. It allowed an entity not associated with Madoff to offer its client a fund that was not only managed by the then 'prestigious' Madoff, but whose assets were also completely handed over to the highly rated Madoff organisation.

Why did the promoters not know that Madoff was abusing this? In effect Madoff did not allow third parties to carry out the required checks on his organisation, so as to avoid anyone finding out he was a fraud. The fact that he was so important in the industry and ran a regulated company helped with the deception. Whether the companies that chose to work with him and so easily relinquished their responsibilities should have acted differently, is another question. I personally think that it was negligence. The defence on which most also rely is that the Madoff fund was sold to willing and knowledgeable investors, and this is backed up by the legal framework under which it was done. Let's look at one example together:

Example: Luxalpha Sicav – American Selection

This was a **UCITS** III fund set up in Luxembourg by UBS and Access Management to feed straight into the Madoff companies.

Looking at the last version of the prospectus for this fund (which is available on the web), you can see the roles of the relevant parties. For example the management company was Access Management Luxembourg and the investment advisor was Access Partners. Referring back to my comments earlier, you can see the live use of the two-tier manager and advisor structure. This in itself raises questions about the credentials of Access Management or Access Partners as asset managers. The custodian and the distributor was UBS (Luxembourg). This role of UBS may have contributed to providing some investors with confidence. Unfortunately the type of contracts that UBS would have had with Luxalpha Sicav would have been written in a way that would allow UBS to disclaim certain liabilities. The auditors were Ernst & Young, again a name that would have provided investors with confidence. The engagement terms of Ernst & Young would have been prepared by it in the way that most auditors prepare them, disclaiming liabilities as much as they can whenever they work from erroneous information. (See Chapter 5 where I go into further detail on the danger of relying too heavily on service providers with a famous name.) The lawyers were a local law firm of good repute. According to this prospectus, the lawyers had one seat on the board of the fund with UBS retaining four. One board seat was held by a member of Access Management. By the look of things an investor could be forgiven for thinking this was a sort of UBS fund.

The prospectus did not, in fact, mention any relationship with any other party, neither BMIS nor any other Madoff entities. Such lack of disclosure and transparency is a good example again of how funds can hide material facts from investors. Presumably, Access Management would have been responsible for explaining the investment strategy to investors. It was not known for its investment work, and as far as I understand it was more of a distribution/marketing company for Madoff products. The set up in itself is not unusual as there are many financial advisors and distributors promoting products to their clients that are managed by selected experts. This is quite common although usually the financial experts (Madoff in this case) are mentioned. Issues relating to custody are rarely explained (so the role of Madoff as a deposit taker would not have been expected to be referred to) simply because the world of custody and sub-custody is traditionally one where sub-custody arrangements are never disclosed. This leaves a massive problem with such a Madoff feeder as the choice of the underlying manager is not explained, and nor was the fact that the assets invested into did not rest with the named custodian of the fund.

What to deduce from a manager's set up

Office space and business organisation

Some managers' or advisors' offices are so extravagant that they make headlines! This is rare but an office can tell you about the style of business management you may be getting involved with. Investors need to understand how managers or advisors establish themselves. This can reveal certain attitudes that can reflect more or less well on the way the business is run and the consequences this could have for your money in the relevant fund.

Managers in London for example are going to be in or around affluent areas such as Mayfair. This is where some of the earlier managers started and the area has become a magnet for the rest. Although it is fine to have this concentration of talent in one area, anyone spending an inordinate amount of money on their office lease to be in this location may not be showing the greatest business sense. I like to visit an office and work out whether it is commensurate in stature with the size of the assets of the relevant fund or client base.

Insurance

Most managers or advisors should have insurance cover, especially professional indemnity (a.k.a. errors and omissions) insurance. This insurance would give them protection against claims for potential mismanagement of the fund's assets. This is significant as the assets in the fund and potential losses are usually many multiples of the assets available to the manager or advisor through its own capital. Taking out insurance cover is not however a legal requirement. Unlike other professionals (such as lawyers) whose regulatory bodies may require some minimum level of insurance this is not the case for managers.

Where managers do have insurance cover, as an investor you should ask for evidence of this, especially as the level of cover may vary widely. Although there is no real benchmark that could help determine what an appropriate level of professional indemnity insurance should be, most firms would tend to have enough insurance cover to insure up to 1 per cent of the overall assets they manage.

IT and business continuity

IT and business continuity should be a key part of any manager's infrastructure. This is relevant to managing market orders, from their initiation to the reconciliation of the cash movements. Business continuity is required of all managers that are regulated in the UK but also makes sense in any case. You want to be sure that the dependency on any one person, or more particularly on any machine or electronic communication system, is correctly addressed. This is done through planning which resources will be deployed in case of an incident or breakdown. You want to know for example that data are backed up and can be reinstated quickly. Such plans can get very technical but can be vital in the case of an emergency. Imagine investing in a firm that breaks down on a 'black swan' rare event day! This could severely hurt performance and lose you a lot of money.

Tax implications of working through the UK

There are some tax risks where a manager or advisor is based in the UK, if it is not properly organised. This should not be ignored by investors in the current context of tax authorities chasing money. Without going into too many technicalities, the offshore structures that rely on a UK manager or an advisor are possibly a risk under English tax laws unless key conditions are met. It is vital that the UK manager or advisor qualifies for certain English tax law exemptions, such as the investment manager exemption (IME), especially where it carries out trading or execution. If the relevant conditions have not been thoroughly considered and complied with by the UK manager or advisor, this creates a risk that the offshore entities may become subject to UK taxation. It also creates a risk for advisors servicing managers who themselves could become the subject of an investigation because of controlled foreign company issues.

It is not the purpose of this book to detail the risks of these structures, but the fiscal context often causes certain structures to follow a defined path and it is therefore my purpose to make sure that investors understand this. Since most fund structures are intricate simply because they consist of numerous entities and individuals in several places, it is wise to investigate and understand their set up, if only to get a sense of how any complexity could affect your money. This helps explain who is actually in control of your money and to what effect. As a general rule I always say that if it is too complicated for you to feel comfortable with then you are probably better off not investing. Just walk away. There should be no shame in avoiding an investment that appears complex to you even if your friends are taking a punt based on disclosed past performance.

Summary

■ Appreciate the structure of the manager you deal with and look at public records including their accounts. It is usually free and very revealing!

■ The manager may be in any number of countries, so check that you understand who does what and where.

■ The people you deal with may not be the only ones with authority over your money. Find out about all relevant roles and responsibilities and check people's backgrounds.

■ The manager's set up – including office, IT and business continuity plan – can be quite revealing. Poor business planning reflects badly on the ultimate business of your selected fund.

2

The fund

What topics are covered in this chapter?

- Investing in a fund
- International legal structure of funds
- Common forms of funds
- Understanding where the money goes
- Fund performance

This chapter focuses on the particularities of the **fund** that is chosen by a potential investor. The fund is ultimately the only party with which the investor will have a contract and in this chapter I seek to break down this relationship to explain not only its relevance but also its limitations.

Investing in a fund

The fund is a legal entity, the main purpose of which is to allow investors to put their money into one pot that can grow under the **manager's** control, free of tax. The fund can be formed in various ways, being a unit trust or a private company for example, or can use the partnership form. It is rare for alternative strategies to be created as unit trust funds.

In effect, therefore, when you invest in most funds you are simply becoming a shareholder and for traditional funds possibly a unit holder.

Unit trust holders tend to have more limited rights. For shareholders, on the other hand, their shareholdings can give them rights akin to those of any other shareholders. Note, however, that when you invest in an **offshore** fund you are almost always issued with non-voting shares, thus ending up with very few rights.

As the name indicates, a non-voting share allows you to take part in the growth and losses of the fund's overall capital, but not to vote on the fund's affairs. This is what frustrated so many investors following the financial crisis as some funds decided almost arbitrarily to suspend the production of **NAVs**, or gated upcoming redemptions of the funds. There was a strong sense of injustice for many investors even if these powers had been disclosed in the legal agreements they had entered into. Investors have sought to argue since then that those agreements were not sufficiently explained to them but that has not won them any favours. We shall talk about the impact of disclosures later in this book. In the meantime it is worth remembering that investors were probably given a false sense of confidence by those selling the virtues of certain funds, with few investors choosing to verify the facts.

It is also worth mentioning at this stage that funds in European jurisdictions, because of different company laws as well as more onerous regulations, would not be able to exclude shareholders in the way that some offshore funds did and thus Europe offers a form of implicit protection. This has meant that more fund business has been driven to Europe since 2008 and I think this trend is bound to continue. The new European laws regarding **UCITS** IV and the AIFMD have both already contributed to this trend.

The fund and the manager are almost one!

- Funds and managers are closely related.
- The reason for this is because of the legislation that applies to funds across the world and which is remote from the public perception that funds are independent.
- In principle a fund is only a pooling vehicle. This is akin to a pot of money that governments recognise as exempt from tax. This is advantageous as only the ultimate gains made by investors are taxed, thus avoiding double taxation that would otherwise impact on the growth of the investments.

▶

■ Legislators felt that this was fair as the idea of pooling money to invest in the economy was overall beneficial to society and encourages people to save, a major issue in western countries. These savings will provide for retirement and pensions.

■ Governments unfortunately only decided to confer this special status on certain types of fund.

■ In Europe the desire to unite these types of funds led to the creation of the UCITS format, a way to harmonise all the relevant funds that should be tax exempt and freely distributable within the EU.

■ When it came to setting up alternative strategies (non-UCITS or equivalent) in the UK for example, no fund format existed. So, most UK-based managers had to create structures outside of the UK, including in the Cayman Islands.

■ Without much of a legal framework, those funds are very much under the control of the manager with few independent safeguards even today.

■ Over the past decade most European countries have created new fund laws to support alternative hedge fund strategies. These fund laws exist for example in Luxembourg and Ireland but also in Spain, Germany and France. The UK has amazingly but willingly stayed out of this space! Despite that, former British Prime Minister Gordon Brown famously sought to blame the Cayman Islands for having hedge funds in its jurisdiction and for the Cayman Islands' presumed role in the 2008 financial crisis. As you can see from the above, it is hardly the Cayman Islands' fault. It just filled a natural vacuum and remains a prime location for hedge funds today.

International legal structures for funds

One of the most important things to understand before you decide to invest in a fund is its legal structure. The legal structure shows you in detail how your money is controlled. It takes a bit of work to comprehend it all, but my aim is to make it easier for you. We are going to start by setting out what you should be looking for. If we all apply this bit of knowledge we will improve the standards of the industry and save you time and money overall.

Focusing on offshore fund structures that use a company form, as this is most common, note that the fund has a **board of directors**. Therefore, some argue that the fund is independent of the manager; however since it has delegated asset management activities to the manager, the main reason for its existence (investing your money) is not within its complete control. The fund does not, in reality – and this is certainly true for offshore hedge funds – deal with its affairs without the approval or guidance of the manager and sometimes the **advisor**, depending on the set up. A fund is almost always set up by those who founded the manager or the advisor. Indeed why would anyone have the incentive of setting up a fund if they are not proposing the management strategy as the essence of the business plan. In effect, therefore, the fund has no real independence from its founders. Both the fund and the manager (and sometimes the advisor) are founded by the same people and/or part of the same group. The commercial purpose and the controls lie with the founders. Even the board of directors of the fund is usually only nominated with the approval of the founders.

Most of the legal structure that is related to the fund and its service providers is therefore controlled by the founders. This starts with the fact that the fund must engage the services of a manager under the terms of a contract, called the **investment management agreement**. The fund's assets are controlled by the manager in accordance with the terms of this agreement. Naturally the founders of the fund will appoint themselves as managers. This approach is logical in the financial industry and what the investor is expecting as well. Investors treat the fund and the manager/advisor as one. They invest on the basis of the investment team they know and meet. Nonetheless this means that the manager will be able to do with the fund almost anything it wants.

In addition, the manager will also usually exercise control over the fund as the main shareholder in it. The fund, notably in the case of an offshore fund, can offer voting shares to the manager, which have the voting rights that investors will not possess. These shares give the manager the power, for example, to remove the board members. You can see that if shares are owned by the manager, the resulting votes and decisions taken by the fund may not, because of this power, necessarily be in your best interests in cases of conflict of interest between the founders and you the investor. This was another source of problems that was crystallised during the financial crisis, when funds took certain decisions that were not those that investors would have preferred, notably when it came to redemptions and giving people their money back.

The manager will also select the fund's other service providers. It will therefore have influence over them, if only because the service providers will have to respect the wishes of whoever gave them work in the first place. The manager is the client in all but name. This could affect the independence of some service providers, such as the banks the administrators or **auditors** who might find it difficult, especially for large clients, to review the pricing of assets or financial statements downwards. This will not happen often but when it does it hurts and usually makes the headlines.

The various international structures of funds can therefore be very revealing if they are understood well, so we now dig into some of the details.

Common forms of funds

Let's consider a few examples of legal structures of funds that you may come across.

Single strategy, single class fund

A single strategy, single class is a simple form of fund structure. From Figure 2.1 you can see that investors' money is pooled into one main fund.

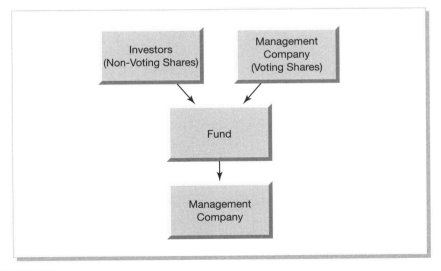

Figure 2.1   Single strategy, single class fund

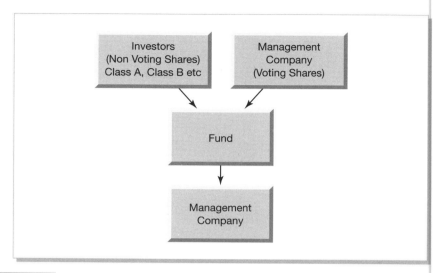

Figure 2.2   Single strategy, multi-class fund

Single strategy, multi-class fund

A single strategy, multi-class fund is similar to a single strategy, single class structure but, as you can see from Figure 2.2, it allows for 'classes' of shares for different investors. In Figure 2.2 there are two share classes on offer, both for the same investment strategy. The purpose of different classes is usually to distinguish between different investors. You can tell share classes apart as they will generally refer to different terms, for example different management fees or different denominations in terms of currency.

I am now going to introduce some more complex structures. These are usually relevant if a fund wants to offer more than one investment strategy. Let's consider what legal structures are available to do this.

Multi-strategy, multi-class fund

Similarly to a single strategy, multi-class fund, a multi-strategy, multi-class fund pools investors from the different classes together (here A and B in Figure 2.3). The manager then feeds the money into two or more investment strategies.

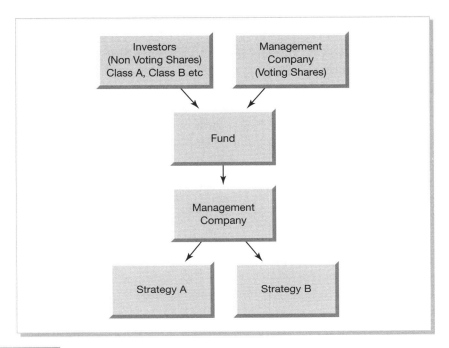

Figure 2.3   Multi-strategy, multi-class fund

This could also be used, for example, to apply different leverage levels to each strategy. Class B could in this case be using more leverage than Class A. Because both classes of shares are in the same actual legal vehicle and are not therefore legally segregated, if one class were to blow up (following a bad investment decision, for example, exacerbated by leverage), the other class's assets would be available to creditors. Therefore, the higher leverage exposure of Class B shares (which could be ruinous in the case of a bad investment) could expose Class A share investors to indirect losses as well.

This potential risk is referred to as **cross-liability** or **contamination** from one fund share class to the next. This form of set up has not been used recently for obvious reasons but older funds may still contain this risk and investors ought to be aware of how to spot it. Without looking at the legal structure, an investor may not even be aware of the other strategy in place under the same fund, which may not be disclosed in marketing materials.

Multi-strategy, multi-class umbrella fund

Cross contamination can be avoided through structuring the fund as a segregated portfolio company (also called a segregated cell company) and more broadly referred to as an **umbrella fund**, a term I shall use in this book. Such umbrella funds can have multiple strategies represented by various sub-funds within the same legal entity. Each sub-fund will have limited liability status with independent profits and losses. The assets of each sub-fund are deemed separate and distinct by the relevant laws of countries where these structures exist. As one legal entity, however, there is only one board and the directors of the umbrella fund have the power to take decisions for each sub-fund.

In Figure 2.4, I show that the main umbrella fund hosts two distinct separate portfolios, represented as Sub-fund A and Sub-fund B. Note that the sub-funds can appoint their own and different managers and service providers if they wish.

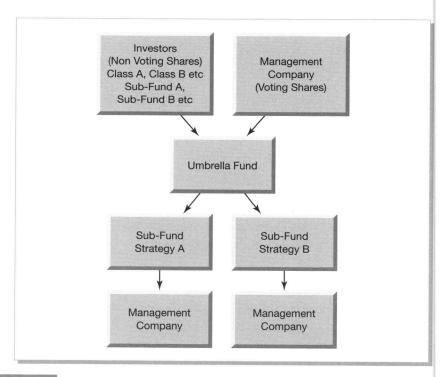

Figure 2.4   Multi-strategy, multi-class umbrella fund

This form of fund is therefore better where there is an aggregation of strategies. Having said that, some people still believe that there is a risk of cross-contamination and prefer to launch a completely separate fund for any new strategy. As far as I know there has been no creditor claim against a group of sub-funds that has been put through a court of law to test the segregation of liability. However, it is probably a good sign that the courts have not been involved, indicating that no cross-contamination claim has been initiated by creditors, presumably because it would be impossible to win a claim for losses in one sub-fund against another within the same umbrella fund.

Other relevant information related to legal fund structures is outlined below in more detail so that you can familiarise yourself with the various types.

The European fund structures

The traditional UCITS fund is the vehicle used in long only asset management. Since this vehicle allows for the use of some derivatives and some leverage these funds can also be used for potential alternative investment strategies. There are currently estimated to be over 400 alternative/hedge fund UCITS compliant funds, and this figure continues to rise. For managers, a major advantage of such UCITS compliant funds is that they can market their units/shares in other EU member states under a simplified procedure usually referred to as the EU Passport.

Note that Europe also allows for less regulated Undertaking for Collective Investment (UCI) funds which are capable of being marketed to retail investors as well as professional and institutional investors. UCIs do not have to comply with the investment restrictions of UCITS and will therefore be subject to more limitations when it comes to passport rights.

An example of a large, so-called alternative UCITS fund is one run by Jabre Capital Partners.

Jabre Capital Partners

Biggest debut for UCITS funds

■ Famous trader Philippe Jabre launched a new fund with Swiss private bank Pictet on 1 February 2010 using manager Jabre Capital Partners.

■ The fund was a convertible bond and multi-strategy fund and attracted €805 million, making it the largest offering in the UCITS fund sector at the time.

■ The fund's strategy was:

  – Invest worldwide with a non-benchmark approach.

  – Seek equity-like returns with lower volatility.

  – Invest primarily in large cap companies based in major global liquid markets, with average exposures of 40 per cent in North America, 40 per cent in Europe and 20 per cent in the rest of the world.

■ The fund was going to charge a 20 per cent performance fee, with no hurdle rate.

Clearly, not all strategies can be structured as UCITS funds. For example, the scope of a global macro strategy will be drastically reduced in a UCITS context, as the fund will not be able to invest in illiquid instruments sometimes favoured by such strategies as they do not fit the daily/weekly liquidity profile required by the UCITS rules. Some managers have still sought to fit their strategy into UCITS rules and this has impacted on the profile of returns, which tend to diverge from those offered by the offshore version of the fund with the same strategy. As a result the UCITS universe is likely to remain limited in comparison to the existing offshore offerings.

The US fund structure

In the US, the rules that apply to mutual funds are not that dissimilar to those that are found in Europe and essentially these protect retail investors. I am not going to review those structures as they do not really affect the life of the European investor. On the other hand many

European investors were exposed to US alternative funds and I would like to briefly mention how those are sometimes relevant. The most common type of fund structure in this context is probably the limited partnership under which the manager is typically the general partner and investors are limited partners. This structure provides a tax benefit to US investors. Very often a fund will have both a US and a non-US structure (again for tax reasons and to satisfy both US and non-US tax regimes). These are often referred to as the **onshore** and offshore structures respectively, as they are seen from a US point of view. We have tended to inherit this language in Europe which can be confusing since a US fund is clearly offshore if you sit in London.

Bearing the above in mind, the US funds, created for US taxpayers, usually feed into an offshore fund. This is known as a master/feeder structure. In this structure, investors therefore invest in a feeder fund which then invests all of its assets into a master fund. From the point of view of European investors this has little impact as they tend to invest directly into an offshore feeder fund or sometimes the offshore master fund and are therefore not concerned with the US directly.

The Caribbean fund structure

There are again many forms of funds in the Caribbean. The ones that are most relevant to this book are based in the Cayman Islands. These are incorporated as limited companies and exempted from regulation by the Cayman Islands Monetary Authority (CIMA). This means that they are very similar to a normal limited liability company, with a board and shareholders. However, because they fall under a certain type of company, it is very common for there to be two types of shares – one with a voting right, the other without. As you read in Chapter 1, the board usually acts on the recommendation of the manager. This means that if the fund wants to change its constitutional documents, for example, it could follow either a board decision and/or the necessary vote from shareholders. In practice an investor will only be buying non-voting shares and will not have any right to vote on any decisions of the fund. This was a main area of concern during the financial crisis, and although some funds did watch out for the wishes of their investors others did not and there was not much that could be done about it. It is also important to understand that the funds are not regulated as such, they are only registered as exempt from regulations. This is often confusing to investors who believe they may be entitled to some form of protection when there is none.

Understanding where the money goes

Behind all of these structures lies more or less the same thing. Investors' money is invested in various underlying assets in accordance with the investment strategy and policy of the fund as stipulated in its **prospectus**. The manager that is responsible for managing the investments can also delegate the responsibility to another manager that will identify the investments and execute the transaction. Alternatively, the manager may seek investment advice from other specialist investment advisors. Where this is the case, the investment advisor(s) will have some responsibility for identifying investments; however, the ultimate decision to make any investment or regarding the direction of the investments should remain with the manager. So far so good ...

The fund itself does not invest its money directly from its own bank account, so in addition to the layers of control above you have to remember that there are other intermediaries that will have an impact on your money. The fund will tend to have a bank account for the receipt of redemptions and subscriptions but the bulk of the cash is transferred to the custodians or in the case of alternative funds to **prime brokers**. This is where the securities are bought for the fund. The fund may have more than one custodian or prime broker and will give rights to the manager's or advisor's staff to instruct the custodian or prime broker to buy or sell positions and route orders through other brokers as necessary. With this in mind the fund money can end up in many places. This explains the Madoff case, where the money of even the most regulated of funds ended up with BMIS (see the Madoff case study in Chapter 1). For other funds this also helps explain why money was lost through Lehman Brothers when that became insolvent. So where the money goes is important and you should be able to work this out from the prospectus; and if not then you should be very concerned. This is why I believe that knowing how to read and understand a prospectus quickly and efficiently is essential for better fund selection. I shall look at this aspect in detail in Chapter 3. In the meantime let's look at what you can do to see if the fund is really making your money work for you.

Fund performance

At the end of the day of course we are all interested in performance and how much money we will make if we invest in a fund and entrust our money to a manager. We also know that past performance is not indicative of future performance. For the purposes of this chapter, however, what I really want to do is assess this past performance and determine what it might tell you about the fund.

Track record

The track record of a fund is its performance over the years and this information is usually one of the easiest and most accessible to obtain. To trumpet monthly returns is the basis of all fund marketing. A long show of data is usually deemed to be a measure of stability and some investors will require a minimum track record of three years or more before they will invest. This is because an established fund with a long track record provides more reliable information on past performance that can be used to evaluate the fund's current position and risk profile, while a fund with little or no track record provides no basis of comparison to evaluate its approach to investing. Though past performance is not indicative of future results, a solid track record grants additional insights into how the fund performs following certain investment decisions and during different economic cycles. However, a track record can be misleading and should be thoroughly checked. For example, sometimes funds will merge the historical performance of more than one fund. Further, the track record of a fund can be the work of various individuals, leading to certain complexities when it comes to understanding who was responsible for the results and whether it was the product of one or more investment professionals.

Remember that the values noted on any factsheet or marketing record depend on the manager alone and are not legally binding even if rules apply as to how they are expressed (see more about that in Chapter 9). It is therefore vital to check such data. This can be done easily by using simple tools like Bloomberg, Reuters or any data sourcing software. Often small mistakes in the track record will give clues about the history of the firm in question or its degree of **compliance** or corporate governance which is insightful when measuring the reliability of the manager as a trusted investment company.

For a practical illustration consider the false track record of Lake Shore Asset Management.

---

case study   Lake Shore Asset Management – a false track record

In brief:

■ Lake Shore Asset Management ('Lake Shore') managed a Chicago-based hedge fund that traded in US commodities futures contracts.

■ Lake Shore claimed to manage $1 billion for investors; however a **CFTC** investigation in 2007 showed that its fund only had approximately $466 million. The CFTC immediately froze $228 million of investors' money.

■ The fund was found to have a false track record and Lake Shore was accused of having delayed providing requested information to the CFTC.

■ The CFTC's findings were that:

– Lake Shore falsely stated that it had generated positive returns since 1993;

– the fund failed to trade at all before 2002; and

– the fund had experienced high trading losses between January 2002 and September 2007.

■ In August 2011, Lake Shore's founder, Philip Baker, pleaded guilty to running a $292 million fraud. He was sentenced to 20 years in prison in the US in November 2011.

Lessons learned

■ Track records may be misleading or false – a simple check on the historical trial balances would have revealed that Lake Shore's track record was unreliable.

I urge you to remain cautious of performance statistics. As noted with Lake Shore you can easily verify the information by asking for the actual financial statements. The more complex the structure of the fund, the more questions you may want to ask to check what the track record actually represents.

Back testing

The track record may also be made up of what is known as back testing, which is a way of showing purported past performance based on the same investment ideas and potential execution but using purely hypothetical data. There are different ways of using this but the first thing an investor should do is ensure the track record is real and preferably audited, which is not always the case. Thereafter if the track record is actually hypothetical, one should keep an open mind as to what it represents in terms of useful information. To properly evaluate such a track record an investor should actually be able to plug in the supposed trades and work backwards to cross check that they match the purported strategy, including all trading costs and the costs of potentially running a fund that are borne and paid out of a fund's assets by investors. In addition, the data for all the trades (their levels, prices which may vary at various times of the day, etc.) should be precise and cross checked accordingly, which is incredibly difficult to do and would monopolise a lot of technical skills. It also assumes transparency from the manager which may be hard to get as usually a new manager will want to protect any trading ideas it has used to make up the track record. All in all, therefore, it is hard to invest on the basis of a track record without full information or an independent audit being performed which is in practice quite rare. That is not to say that you should avoid entrepreneurial strategies based on back testing; instead consider the relevant risks as larger than normal and allocate your investment accordingly.

Targets

When assessing performance we tend to look at the published NAVs. However don't rely only on actual historical performance but understand a manager's original targets. This is a simple little trick but ask a manager for its target returns and risks (usually measured as volatility). Many have a target return but no target for risk ... I always find that interesting and very disappointing. How can a manager not have an idea of risk targets? It is a bit like a Formula 1 driver knowing how fast he can go but not thinking of how soon he should slow down ahead of a sharp corner.

If you get hold of targets, they allow you to check whether the manager does actually meet them. Again this is easy to determine and often very revealing of whether the manager is actually delivering. The reality is that as much as markets are unpredictable, so are targets, but it will give you an idea of the manager's ambitions as well as its relative appreciation of how hard targets are to meet if they are set too high.

Still using targets, I find it very telling to compare them with any older targets that might be stated in prior presentations, older documents or websites. This may actually reveal that a few years back the targets were different and if so the manager should explain why. Usually that is related to either the markets changing or to a change in the investment strategy. Again any change in itself is not necessarily an issue, but it does indicate a potential change of trading style and this has to be understood. It also allows you to determine whether the manager is actually successful in implementing one style of strategy over time.

Correlation issues

I ought to note here that performance should not be looked at on its own, but should always be linked to a form of risk measure. Most investors know to look at performance in terms of ratios that account for risk. However, another theme which is just as important for me is that the performance must also be assessed in the context of other investment strategies. Indeed many funds might show good returns in good times, but likewise will be affected by the losses that hit the markets when things are bad. This is a matter of correlation. This statistical information is crucial and is not easy to obtain or to use. Not all correlation measures for example compare apples to apples. Some compare a fund's performance to the equity markets, others are more interested in comparing the fund's performance against that of other funds. Other forms of analysis look at the correlation of the fund to sectorial indexes only. In my view unless you are seeking a specialised analysis, you should be concerned mainly with the correlation of a fund to the equity markets as this is where in all likelihood your other investments, like your pension fund, will be invested. It is therefore important that overall you know how much exposure you have to the equity markets. Peer correlation or correlation to a specific sectorial index is really only useful for specialists who may need to know the actual relationship between a manager's strategy and that sector. The aim for most investors is to reduce their overall exposure to equity and sometimes bond funds which they will presumably hold in their portfolios. In fact I am still dumbfounded by the fact that so many professional advisors plugged so many investors into correlated strategies be they alternative or not, through to 2008. Having said that, although I stress the point on correlation and would rather have low but de-correlated returns, many de-correlated strategies are either complex or do not provide much return as opposed to the more volatile equity sector, and are therefore not popular. This was true before 2008 and is still true today. Furthermore, although investors hope for de-correlation on the down side, they generally want correlation on the way up.

Summary

- A fund is a legal entity that allows investors to put money in one pot which can grow free of tax.

- International legal structures for funds show how your money is controlled.

- Look into the common forms of funds that you are likely to come across.

- Understand where the money goes – the underlying assets, the manager and other parties involved.

- Past performance can show you a lot about the fund or manager. To understand it properly look at the track record, back testing, targets and correlation issues.

3

The prospectus

What topics are covered in this chapter?

- Why is there a prospectus?
- Leverage and investment restrictions
- Fees
- The subscription and redemption forms in the prospectus
- Corroboration and gap analysis with marketing material

Although often treated as a long, bulky and boring document, the **prospectus**, also called the 'offering memorandum' or the 'private placement memorandum' (see the Glossary for a fuller explanation), is very useful and can be read quite quickly if you know what you are looking for. Most prospectuses follow a similar format which makes them easy to review. The details vary though so reading some parts carefully will reveal a variety of more or less relevant risks. It is amazing how, as a source of information, and as a contract with investors, prospectuses are nonetheless hardly used by investors. In reality the prospectus is the only true and legal link between an investor and a **fund**. I believe that investors do not understand that fully, and fail to dissociate the agreement they have with the fund, through the subscription form which is directly connected to the prospectus, from the promises made through various representations by the **managers** which are not legally binding. It is also the reason for the frustration felt during the financial crisis by so many investors, as there was a clear divide between expectations based on oral statements and marketing presentations as opposed to the harsher reality expressed in writing in relevant prospectuses. My aim in this chapter is ambitious. I want to make a prospectus likeable and a very useful read.

Why is there a prospectus?

The prospectus is written by the fund's lawyers under the usual influence of the manager, as I explained earlier. By definition therefore it is not designed to offer investors any protection unless that protection is afforded by a law that imposes restrictions. This is the case for regulated funds but it is quite the opposite for non-regulated funds. To be even clearer, the prospectus is designed to 'protect the traders' as a banker once said to me. It does a wonderful job of it too ... so read it, even if you cannot change it, so you are aware of how bad things might become for you. At least if investors all read prospectuses and complained as to how soft these documents are when it comes to investor protection, maybe standards would improve!

For regulated funds, the main difference is that the prospectus is controlled (to a degree only) by law and must include language about investor safeguards regarding for example diversification and limits on borrowing and leverage. That is the fundamental difference between a fund's prospectus based in the Cayman Islands and a regulated fund's prospectus based in Europe.

The majority of prospectuses are, whatever the jurisdiction, drafted with more favourable terms for the manager and the fund. They are a product of the manager and are not designed to protect investors, except under certain regulatory regimes as noted above, but even that is not as far reaching as you might think. The description of the investment strategy, for example, tends to be quite flexible and open, so that the manager can, as much as possible, buy whatever assets it chooses. This is helpful of course should the strategy need to be diversified or changed, but some investors would prefer to know what is going to be in the portfolio. The flexibility afforded by the prospectus also means that the manager can do as it sees fit and not be accountable to investors should the selected new assets prove to be risky and/ or valueless over time.

So be sure to read the clauses in the prospectus in context and review them in line with other documentation available externally so as to cross check information. This can be done using the **due diligence questionnaire (DDQ)**, marketing presentations, monthly fact sheets, or by checking **prime broker** statements and trial balances for example, to note any assets that may be held but that do not match the generic descriptions and limitations noted in the prospectus or in the marketing documentation, or indeed the level of leverage used. This is of course particularly relevant for unregulated funds.

Quick tips on how to approach a prospectus

1 Know that the prospectus is designed to spell out risks, so that you cannot pretend that you were unaware of the things that can go wrong. So, read a prospectus with an inquisitive, sceptical and assertive frame of mind.

2 Remember that most of the prospectuses you read will say the same things. Use that to save time and avoid reading the obvious sections. On the other hand look for gaps in information.

3 Get an understanding of all the parts of the prospectus by looking at the table of contents and use that to identify where you will focus.

4 Note that it may be easier to read a prospectus electronically as you can easily go to the sections that are of interest using the simple search functions available when reading computer documents.

5 In the prospectus look for the description of the investment strategy – is it realistic? Is it very broad and non-descriptive? Does it reflect what you have been told?

6 Consider the fund's board members, normally described in the prospectus. See that you are comfortable with their backgrounds and their independence. The **board of directors** can be influenced by the manager so form a view that is realistic in this context.

7 Consider the description of the manager and its key people – these are the people who will be investing your money.

8 Consider the description of the service providers (banks, brokers, accountants, lawyers) and check independently that they are still appointed and working with the fund. There are historical instances where prime brokers ceased to work for a fund without that being reflected in the prospectus.

9 Consider the clauses on valuation of assets. Note that almost always these clauses do not give you much detail on how hard-to-value assets will be calculated nor do they put the responsibility for getting the price on anyone specifically. This means you have no recourse if things go wrong.

10 Consider the descriptions made in relation to redemptions and payment timeframes in particular.

11 Review anything to do with fees so that you find out if there are 'hidden' charges.

12 Finally review aspects of potential suspension of redemptions and/or gating provisions. As far as I have seen all funds have some form of right to limit redemptions.

Leverage and investment restrictions

Leverage restrictions may hold less value than their title suggests when it comes to **offshore** funds. Sometimes they are silent on the subject; more often they include very loose restrictions designed to leave the manager a lot of flexibility should leverage be used. Professional investors have said to me that this is normal and quite acceptable, but in my view this is not right. It is not because we trust managers that we have to give them *carte blanche*. I think all prospectuses should have a limit on leverage. If the manager wants to increase leverage then it should inform investors and notify them if leverage limits are breached. That would at least give investors the right to decide to redeem if they prefer. If it is not in the prospectus an investor simply has no right to know.

Most prospectuses include some form of investment restrictions that investors may seek to rely on. These can be based on the standard investment restrictions required, as I said, in the relevant jurisdiction (if any) where the fund is set up or depending on its targeted base of investors. For instance, generally retail funds must include by law more restrictions such as limited exposure to any one stock to control concentration risks. Other restrictions that are sometimes seen are based on those required for a listing: often in Europe this applies in Ireland. All restrictions are good, although I have known of funds that simply chose to ignore them. It is rare but if it happens in an offshore jurisdiction with a dishonest manager it is hard for investors to do much about it without incurring huge costs.

case study   ## Confessions of a prospectus writer

There are a number of examples in the industry where the prospectus includes clauses that directly prejudice investors. I want to illustrate them so that investors can easily pick up on aspects of prospectuses they should resist. These examples are related to offshore unregulated funds which are the funds investors are most likely to struggle with. They are also often the funds that make the press for related reasons.

Although I did not write any of the prospectuses that contain the examples below, I can understand what those who did were trying to achieve. Let me tell you therefore about the consequences for investors in each case.

Example 1

Here is an example of language that could be included in a prospectus with regards to leverage:

Snapshot of the prospectus...

Leverage from derivatives

The share of the stock exchange margins on the total fund volume shall not exceed 35 per cent. This could lead to a one-sided use of the margin limit at a maximum leverage effect out of derivatives of up to 12 times the actual fund volume (i.e. 1,200 per cent).

Total leverage of the fund

The expected leverage of investments in higher risk markets (such as raw material, precious metal, energy) of the fund's total leverage is 5-8 times the actual fund volume. The maximum possible leverage of an exemplary investment (long only) in risky markets may be up to 15 times the fund volume, i.e. the basic equivalent volume of the invested options and futures would be up to 15 times higher than the actual fund volume.

Leverage is a very important topic and the cause of much of the financial pain felt in 2008. Interestingly in 1998 leverage was also a primary concern when the famous Long Term Capital Management (LTCM) fund collapsed bringing to the brink many large financial institutions (see Chapter 7 for the full story of LTCM). Yet, as you can read below, not much has changed over a decade in the way leverage is referred to in many prospectuses, leaving far too much freedom to managers. Leverage is still, even as I write in 2012, rarely limited in prospectuses or if it is, it is at levels that do not protect investors enough, unless of course you are in a regulated European fund.

In effect in the language used here, the fund is pretty free to leverage under two clauses to quite scary levels! The reality is that the fund probably does not use this level of leverage. Nevertheless, investors should wonder why such broad and relatively unlimited clauses are included in prospectuses in the first place. The fact remains that if funds use such clauses the risk is on the investor. To be fair some strategies may need this freedom, but if it is essentially an equity long short fund it certainly does not need the powers to leverage on such things as raw materials! From my point of view this should stand out as poor drafting and a total lack of care for investors.

Example 2

This example is relevant to valuation issues:

Snapshot of the prospectus...

> The valuation of a security listed or traded on an official stock exchange or other regulated market operating regularly and open to the public is based on the last available price of the date preceding the valuation date. If this security is traded on several markets, the valuation will be done on the basis of the last price known on the market considered to be the main market for trading this security. If the last known price is not appropriate, *the valuation shall be based on the probable realisation value estimated by the board of directors of the fund with prudence and in good faith*.

Typically valuation is a dangerous area which I believe is tremendously significant but often disregarded by investors. The financial crisis of 2008 certainly revealed this. In this example the key phrase is emphasised. Basically it suggests that where a valuation may be hard to obtain, the board of directors should use the price they deem fair, acting with prudence and good faith. This leaves the board a lot of room for manoeuvre. Even if it is perceived as a fair system it is certainly not the best. As I explained in Chapter 1, the manager will be influential on that board of directors. In practice the fund will also ask that the indication of price, for hard to value assets, is typically given by the manager. The conflicts of interest that we identified earlier become immediately relevant. This is exactly what happened in many cases in 2008. The board, however, is not acting unreasonably by relying on the manager according to the industry and therefore will be pretty much blameless even if wrong. Investors do not always understand this established relationship. Further, investors often believe that in such a case the **administrator**, who is perceived to be the accountant of the fund, will be responsible for calculating the **NAV** of the fund. They believe therefore that the administrator would confirm the reasonableness of the relevant price. This would indeed help alleviate the problems I have highlighted. Yet, the administrator does not have this legal responsibility. If the assets are hard to price the administrator too would rely on the manager's price. As such they will fall directly into the conflict of interest pitfall! Now, if all directors of funds were acting with sufficient resources and could therefore diligently verify a price given to them, the language in this example would not be an issue. But as it stands and in the context I have given, it is not enough to protect investors. There is simply too much room for conflict, and too lax a control as the job of pricing assets is onerous.

In Chapter 5 I talk about the administrator in more detail and review its actual duties to the fund and responsibilities to investors.

Example 3

This last example deals with the potential suspension of redemptions, a nightmare in 2008 and 2009 for many investors:

Snapshot of the prospectus...

> If, in the opinion of the directors, the key man becomes disabled, deceased or otherwise incapable or unwilling to dedicate the majority of their professional efforts to the manager, the directors will promptly notify all shareholders. During the 30-day period (the 'key man period') following notice of such an event, **redemptions will be suspended** so as to allow for an orderly transition in the investment management of the fund.

This clause is interesting and in this case it may be argued that it might present some advantages for investors, as it considers the probability that in the case of the incapacity of the manager the fund would suspend redemptions. This may avoid a disorderly sequence of redemptions and protect the value of the assets in the fund. However, it is also an investor's prerogative to redeem on such an event happening. You might also assume that if a fund is so largely dependent on one man then that in itself is a risk not worth taking. As I have said before read the clause in context but do not ignore it. It is telling you something and possibly the lawyers who drafted it know something about the fund or the manager that you don't. Another point is to think about the clause in the context of the strategy. If the fund is using a liquid strategy, as it was here, then there is no reason to block redemptions. In equity long short unless the fund is dealing in small capitalisation stocks it should be able to close out positions easily and let investors redeem if they so wish.

Fees

When reviewing the prospectus, it is useful to consider the different types of fees. This will not only confirm the charges which you as an investor should already know about, but can overall give an indication of the attitude of those behind the fund towards protecting your money… I always think that an honest and concerned manager will, through the prospectus, show that it means to treat investors fairly. Excessive fees on the other hand reflect a certain attitude that I consider unhelpful, and in addition will lessen returns that are calculated net of fees.

When looking at the fee levels you should first focus on the management and performance fees. You should consider whether they or other fees are reasonable or so high that they unnecessarily eat up performance overall. The best measure of this is the **total expense ratio (TER)**. This will help you determine that you are not paying more than you should. Remember that there are neither rules nor laws on the types of fees that are included in a fund. So you have to rely on your own assessment and the prospectus is a good place to start.

Here are a few things to look out for in relation to general industry standards.

Management fees

Management fees are fees charged by the manager for the general management of the fund, generally 2 per cent of NAV for alternative strategies and 1 per cent for traditional long only strategies.

Some funds have recently lowered these fees in response to angry investors that felt they had overpaid for management services that did not protect against the heavy market losses of 2008. Other funds still maintain high management fees, sometimes as high as 3 per cent. This is either due to popularity or sometimes in the case of funds that invest in futures, the management fee is linked to the leverage that occurs through gearing.

In my view funds can be evaluated based on whether their fees are aligned with general industry standards. A fund that is either more expensive or cheaper deserves further enquiries. High management fees mean that managers will be making money no matter how the fund performs and this could therefore decrease the incentive for managers to create gains.

Performance fees

Performance fees are fees charged by the manager for increases in the fund's NAV, generally at 20 per cent for alternative strategies and less often at 10 per cent for traditional strategies if they charge performance fees at all (they did not use to but many do now).

Sometimes this fee is limited thanks to the use of a **hurdle rate** or **high water mark**. A hurdle rate is a level of return that the fund must exceed before it can claim its performance fee. A high water mark is even fairer for investors in that much like the water level on the river, the fund can only be paid performance fees if it is above the last highest NAV reached since its inception. Sometimes the high water mark is reset every year, which is clearly not as good for investors and should be picked up from the prospectus.

Note that after the financial crisis, some managers worried that they had lost so much performance that they would not be paid a performance fee again for a long time. They therefore went about amending the prospectus to reset the high water mark. This was a clever commercial move but for investors it is a bit like moving the goal posts during the game because the game has become too hard.

Subscription/redemption fees

These are additional charges applied usually to new subscriptions or when redeeming an investment. I think of them as a form of penalty. They are quite rare in the alternative fund industry and are not in line with industry standards. They are however quite traditional for long only funds (usually to pay for financial companies that act as intermediaries bringing their clients into the funds). Since the two forms of strategies are merging and we are seeing pressure being applied to management fees my guess is that they are likely to pick up! Therefore

caution should be exercised when such fees are referred to in the prospectus. They were usually used to pay for intermediary distribution
services or to make sure that investors do not 'trade' the fund by going
in and out depending on their own economic assessment of the general strategy. I do not like them much, especially as I know that they
can be waived for some investors, which means that it leads to potential favouritism and that it creates more conflicts for the manager. Be
alert as the subscription fees can sometimes be referred to as sales fees
or distribution fees.

Other fees

Sometimes the prospectus will have a section entitled 'other fees'
or something similar and worded in such a loose way that you may
not immediately spot it. This is designed to add new fees and in my
view is rarely justified ... what it usually seeks to include are fees that
should, in my view, be paid by the manager from its own management fees. These can include shareholder service fees for the manager,
or the reimbursement of broad expenses such as travelling costs or
Bloomberg stations.

Who receives the fees? The manager or the fund

Note that some of the fees discussed in this section might be assumed
to be paid to the fund, thus benefiting all investors. You can check
this as it is not always the case, and sometimes fees just fill up the
manager's coffers. If the fees are paid into the fund for the benefit of
its overall investors then I would consider them neutral. The other
fee I would accept is that which may be retained by a fund after you
redeem and which is used to guarantee that all investors contribute
fairly to the costs of the fund, not just those left in at year end. You do
not want only the last few investors to be stuck with the legal costs of
a fund liquidation! Trust me this happens and then the last investor is
mightily annoyed and the manager who forgot to think ahead pretty
embarrassed as well as potentially liable for liquidation fees.

The subscription and redemption forms in the prospectus

Subscriptions

An investor will invest in a fund by way of a subscription which in reality is done through a document that will set out a variety of information, notably how much is invested and in which share class. This will be accompanied by much legal jargon in relation to anti-money laundering information (requiring full details of the investor). The details of when and how an investor can subscribe in a fund are set out in the prospectus and the subscription document is the contractual realisation that you as the investor will have with the fund. This is essentially your only contract with the fund. Depending on the manager's preference, subscription documents may either be presented as part of the prospectus or as a separate document.

I always remind people that only this contract regulates the relationship of the investor with the fund. Also remember that there are minimum investment levels. Usually there is an initial and subsequent minimum investment amount that is allowed. Check if the fund is for only the very wealthy or is more broadly offered.

Always think of your entry. Usually funds will closely regulate the period of entry and the required notice you must give to the fund. Frequency and required notice periods are also valuable information for investors and a special note should be made if any fees are charged on entry by the fund or any intermediary. This will have an impact on the amount invested and the cost to the investor.

The frequency of exit will have an impact on the liquidity of the investment and, as we saw during the financial crisis, even when there is a stated liquidity period this is not guaranteed as the prospectus will often contain clauses that allow the fund to change this pretty much as it sees fit.

Redemptions

Redemption policies can have a big impact on the marketability of the fund. Redemption frequency and notice periods determine the liquidity of an investor's investment, as they affect the time period during which money is held up in a fund. As I mentioned previously, the right to redeem is part of the contract with the investor and is set out in the prospectus but in most cases the wording of the relevant clauses will be highly favourable to the fund. This wording should not just be checked but thoroughly understood by investors therefore.

When liquidity dried up during the financial crisis many investors complained of being gated. It is easy to have sympathy for them as they were probably told during oral marketing presentations that they would have access to their money with relative ease. Unfortunately the truth was that they got stuck because when markets are not normal liquidity dries up. The harsh reality is that investors have only themselves to blame (unless they were wrongly advised by an interme-diary) as sophisticated investors are deemed to be able to understand the degree of legal control they have when they sign up to a prospec-tus. I cannot help note that there is a degree of hypocrisy revealed when, not so much the sophisticated individual investors, but rather sophisticated corporate professional investors such as funds of funds, claim that they have missed this point of detail.

Other aspects of the fund that must be considered when looking at a future redemption are any clauses in the prospectus on hard and soft lock-ups as these will also influence the fund's liquidity. Hard lock-ups require investors to keep their money invested for a predetermined period of time before it is eligible for redemption. Soft lock-ups allow investors to withdraw money from the fund, but an additional fee or penalty will be charged within certain predetermined minimum periods. There is nothing wrong with such rules, which are normally designed to protect an overall strategy that may not be best served if investors can come in and out as they please. However they may not always be reflected clearly in marketing presentations and this emphasises the point that investors must take a detailed look at every prospectus.

Corroboration and gap analysis with marketing material

A valuable tip! Check information from the marketing materials and cross check it against the prospectus. A fund's marketing material usu-ally highlights its key benefits, notably showing off its investment strategies, key personnel, past performance, and operating policies and practices. While this information, provided by the manager, is beneficial for potential investors, there is a strong bias to make funds sound good and few legal obligations not to exaggerate or, dare I say it, mislead investors.

case study   # Caught in the act of marketing

Fund X has a hypothetical prospectus stating that there are no limits to leverage. The marketing materials for fund X, which were used in presentations to sell the fund to new investors, contradict the prospectus. Such marketing materials claim that the fund will be leveraged at a maximum of 2½ times the value of the assets. Here the marketing materials lure investors into a false sense of security that the fund has limited leveraging:

Snapshot of fund X's prospectus…

Borrowing of cash and securities and certain loans; short sales

The fund is permitted to borrow for the purposes of providing liquidity to fund redemptions by shareholders and/or for investment purposes, subject to regulatory requirements and for the payment of fees, expenses and other short-term fund obligations. There are *no limits* to the fund's borrowing ability…

Compare the above to the fund's hypothetical marketing material which advocates that there is a limitation on gross exposure:

Snapshot of fund X's marketing presentation…

Forecasted exposures

Number of positions	35 to 50
Gross exposure	Average 185%, between 85% and 250%
Net exposure	Average 25%, between −40% and 85%
Geography	Average 40% North America, 40% Europe, 20% Other

Investors might not catch on to subtle but crucial differences between the marketing material and prospectus. Nevertheless, the responsibility lies with the investor to read the prospectus as it is this, not the marketing material, that is legally binding for the fund. Legally investors would find it very hard, if not impossible, to sue on the basis of misrepresentations made in such documents!

Another useful source of information for corroboration and gap analysis is the **DDQ** (sometimes for long only funds the equivalent is the request for proposal) that funds and managers prepare and distribute to investors. The DDQ is designed as a more factual summary of key questions regarding the fund and the manager. It provides more in-depth information than the general marketing presentations or indeed the prospectus but is *not* legally binding! This is why you must compare it to the legally binding prospectus.

Overall, therefore, it is crucial for prospective investors to compare fund information from multiple documents provided by the manager. Do not rely on any marketing material or the DDQ alone. Any inconsistencies between the marketing material, DDQ and prospectus should be noted and be used to ask the manager pertinent questions. For example, I came across one fund in which the prospectus stated an inception date that differed quite significantly from the inception date outlined in the fund's marketing materials (newsletters) which was much shorter. As a result, part of the track record was not included in the fund's monthly fact sheets, and in this case that made the fund look a lot better than it actually was.

Summary

- The prospectus is a long document but it is essential that investors read it as it is the legal link between an investor and a fund.

- Understand the subscription and redemption forms.

- Cross check marketing materials and DDQs against the prospectus.

4

Governance

What topics are covered in this chapter?

- Key individuals
- Organisation of employees
- Directors' independence
- Management dedication

The management of any company, including a **manager** or an **advisor,** is human-led and naturally subject to the actions and omissions of its staff. In line with regulations but also common decency, such staff should act in a way that is conducive to protecting and growing your money. I believe that corporate governance is therefore vital and should help provide a reliable framework around those with relevant duties. You can find out about corporate governance inside a company relatively easily as it should be reflected in a well-organised business, with governance being taken seriously from the top to the bottom. The regulators quite clearly expect senior management to be responsible. Therefore investors should push to get the relevant information about anyone interacting with their money.

In the context of managers/advisors, things that matter to me include evidence that proper meetings take place to discuss asset management and more importantly risk management. It is always a plus to see that in writing otherwise, from my experience, I know that it is unlikely to be happening. If meetings are not taken seriously enough, it is likely that they are not happening with sufficient regularity to ensure the continuous monitoring of risks. I also believe that where a meeting takes place, if it is recorded, however briefly, it makes the business more efficient and progressive as it is more likely to review past decisions and actions to remedy issues.

Key individuals

Since a company is led from the top and in financial management in particular you are dependent on the proper character of those that handle your money, the first thing to do when dealing with **funds** is to know who you are dealing with. You might have noticed that the common practice is to be told very little about who runs a fund, except perhaps for the names of the potential star managers and the most prominent aspects of their history. Investors are used to this and assume that the lowest level of disclosure is fine when it comes to entrusting their money to strangers. Yet every individual at a manager will have a bearing on what happens to the fund's money, in particular those persons dealing with placing orders and/or executing the orders of the manager, and those responsible for stopping trades and controlling risks. These individuals not only control what happens to investments but also what happens to the cash in the portfolio.

The key individuals representing the fund, the manager or the advisor would include senior management, usually the Chief Executive Officer (CEO), the Chief Investment Officer, the Chief Operating Officer and the directors (sometimes these are the same persons). Other key individuals are those within the investment management team. These are the main decision makers notably with regards to the movement of any money. Finally I would add the risk management team as it is the only internal protection you have. It is therefore necessary to understand the way the manager, advisor and fund are organised, in terms of business management, asset management and risk management on the one hand, and in terms of front office, middle office and back office on the other. It is equally relevant to check that key individuals are organised according to a structure that reflects proper controls.

I believe that you should always start by carefully considering the background of the team you are entrusting your money to. There is always a description of the background of the main principals, either in the **prospectus** or in the DDQ. This should give you an indication of prior expertise and help you assess the team's true abilities. You can even cross check this information with what is available from public sources (see Chapter 10 on background checks). There are immediate risks that can be avoided this way. Another way to access revealing information on some of the key individuals is to ask for personal references. Most people will have standard pre-written references on file but there is also the possibility of talking directly with any prior colleagues or employers. This is always a good step to take, even if it takes a bit of time, as it almost always gives invaluable insights. If you are just a small investor in a large fund this may not be possible, although remember that nothing stops you from trying.

All key individuals should have, as part of their duties and sometimes as a result of their **compliance** obligations, certain responsibilities varying from the process of asset management to recruitment. Organising the manager's life is not simple. As in any business, there are plenty of operational complexities. Ultimately, you must be assured that the person responsible for the relevant operations is capable of carrying out their duties. Otherwise something will inevitably go wrong.

These kinds of operational structures should be enforced by senior management whose ultimate duty is to ensure the business is well run. If this is missed the likelihood of problems is much greater and in fact most issues start from weak management.

In the case of the manager Sextant Capital Management there were plenty of corporate governance issues, one of which was that the sole signatory on the custody accounts of three of the main funds that the company managed was Otto Spork, the main principal. Perhaps if investors had checked this they might have questioned other aspects of Sextant's corporate governance which could have put them on alert regarding the risk of potential fraud. As it was, it was the Canadian regulator that uncovered this remarkable fraud.

Sextant Capital Management

In brief:

■ Former dentist Otto Spork set up a private investment vehicle in 2006 called Sextant Strategic Opportunities Hedge Fund.

■ By November 2008, Sextant boasted a 730 per cent return since its inception.

■ The fund had raised a total of $53 million by then.

■ Canada's Ontario Securities Commission (OSC) conducted a routine compliance review in December 2008 which found that Spork and Sextant Capital Management had perpetrated a fraud in three ways:

  – Its funds were sold at falsely inflated values: Spork inflated the value of the shares by about 1,340 per cent.

  – Spork took millions of dollars in fees based on those falsely inflated values.

  – Spork directly misappropriated money from investors' funds. Approximately 95 per cent of the assets of the Sextant fund were invested illegally in two private companies with ownership stakes in Icelandic glaciers and which were controlled by Spork.

■ Spork's partner in the firm, Konstatinos Ekonomidis, was his brother-in-law; and Spork's daughter was Sextant's president.

■ Spork was authorised as a sole signatory on the custody accounts of Sextant's three main funds and allegedly made a number of transfers to his own personal holding company which amounted to a value in excess of $4 million between 2007 and 2008.

■ Spork denies any wrongdoing, and has vowed to fight the charges.

The path for greater safety

■ Consider that the ability to move money as a sole signatory is always a great risk.

■ Consider the involvement of family members as requiring more scrutiny as there are always resulting allegiances; although some are very honest too many have failed the test.

■ Be cautious of the lack of previous relevant work experience – Spork was a dentist prior to setting up Sextant Capital Management.

> Clearly in the case of Sextant corporate governance was weak in many respects. Yet like many frauds it is hard to uncover the actual abuses before it is too late. I think a review of corporate governance issues would have highlighted enough problems for investors to either invest less or not invest at all.

Investigating the standards of corporate governance is not hard. You should easily be able to check who the official signatories are from company records if they are publicly available and, where they are not, there is no legitimate reason for the manager or the advisor to withhold any such information from you. If you want to double check what the manager is telling you this is easy too. You can ask to review previous copies of banking instructions or company minutes origi- nally granting this type of authority. This is also part of the corporate powers that any broker would usually want to see before opening an account, so you can ask to see what was given to brokers.

The best approach to understanding who should be checked more thoroughly is to follow the hierarchy of the manager or advisor's teams from founders to back office staff. Let me explain how the teams in a manager or advisor are usually organised.

Organisation of employees

The manager or advisor will commonly have employees across the fol- lowing eight areas:

1 portfolio management

2 risk management

3 investment research and analysis

4 investor relations

5 legal and compliance

6 accounting

7 front to back office

8 IT.

Note that not all managers or advisors will have the resources to fill in all those positions. Nonetheless, to properly assess the capacities of managers or advisors let's look into what each department would cover in terms of roles and responsibilities:

1 Portfolio management. This is pretty obvious and, as expected, relevant employees will, depending on their level of seniority, have the right to trade the assets of the fund. They can therefore take positions depending on the total level of assets and in connection with the relevant strategy. Their work should be controlled by risk management.

2 Risk management. This is a key part of the business of asset management which can sometimes be combined with the portfolio management team but should be completely independent. Risk managers should also have the same authority as the most senior asset managers. In most cases risk managers do their job once they find out what has been done by the asset managers. They therefore look at risk after portfolio positions have been bought and sold. Risk managers are then responsible for alerting asset managers where they consider that certain positions expose the fund to too much risk. They must take the required actions to limit or cut risk. Where risk managers are involved earlier and have access to pre-trade potential orders this can allow them to prevent trading mistakes much more readily.

3 Investment research and analysis. This team is usually a support team to the asset managers and is used to find information on which they will trade. A strong research team will often reinforce a well organised portfolio management team that uses fundamental analysis more than a team that uses technical analysis. This is because fundamental investors rely a lot on larger economic studies whilst technical traders, as the name suggests, work from charts showing technical data relating to the volume and prices of financial instruments traded.

4 Investor relations. This team helps with managing the investors, either new ones or existing ones. It usually promotes information on the managers' success and disseminates performance information for the fund. What they say should be taken with caution as the manager or advisor is contractually and legally protected by disclaimers. You should be aware of that and read the relevant small print and the prospectus.

5 Legal and compliance. Often made up of lawyers or accountants this team deals with the contractual aspects of the life of a manager/advisor and ongoing compliance obligations. At times it is very useful to find out how much hands-on experience this team actually has, especially since their involvement in the business of the company should, in practice, avoid many problems.

6 Accounting. This is usually a reference to bookkeeping. The manager or advisor like any other business has to produce accounts and if regulated has to be audited. This involves keeping the books, dealing with the profit and loss accounts and balance sheet items. This is not related to the fund at all. It is important to understand this segregation. The accounts of the manager are rarely looked at by many investors, but they can reveal a lot of information about the business management amongst other things.

7 Front to back office. This is a term that seeks to group the front office (traders) and back office (operations) personnel who are responsible for verifying that the trades of the asset managers are properly recorded by the relevant banks. They also check that the securities are therefore held by the fund and paid for. The responsibilities have expanded from mere reconciliation of orders to progressively handling more of the responsibilities that pertain to the movement of cash, dealing with exchange rate issues and so on. Much of that is driven by electronic communication between the manager, the banks and the **administrator** of the fund. In addition this team assists with the 'shadow' calculation of the fund's **net asset value**. They take information available from the fund's service providers and work out the value of the fund at a set date. They also confirm the amount of cash the asset managers will have to invest on a day-to-day basis.

8 IT. This is a vital support function and will help sustain the information flows between the various parts of the business. In addition this team is responsible for the business continuity and disaster recovery processes of the company. IT and business continuity are key to the operations of a company. Proper business continuity plans are also required of all firms regulated in the UK, for example. Business continuity ensures that the dependency on any one person, or more particularly on any machine or electronic communication system for certain investment strategies, is correctly addressed. This is done through planning which resources will be deployed in the case of a disaster or the failure of key systems. As an investor, you might want to know, for example, that key data pertaining to the investment strategy of the fund are backed up and quickly accessible at another location, in case of a disaster. Such plans can get very technical but can be vital in an emergency. Imagine investing in a firm that experiences a key failure or a disaster on a 'black swan' rare event day! This could severely harm performance and lose you a lot of money.

Common checks on the manager or advisor can be made in respect of which employees do what jobs. They should be easily accessible notably for regulated companies which must keep internal information on the roles and responsibilities of their staff. You can ask to review the organisational chart, for example, which should include their positions and the areas they cover. This allows you to confirm how roles are segregated where relevant. For instance, is the risk manager or compliance officer (or the persons with such roles) acting independently from the asset management team? Are they truly influential in the organisation? For example, are there instances they can recall when they took action that stopped an investment decision?

In addition investors should look for potential conflicts of interest, such as the remuneration structure, to understand how certain team members are compensated and where their interest may therefore lie. Even though there are now rules on remuneration policies for regulated firms in Europe, it is not clear what effect the rules will actually have in practice. What is certain is that if a risk manager disagrees with the investment decision of a senior asset manager, who also decides the risk manager's bonus, it is fair to say that the risk manager is not likely to act independently.

I strongly advise you to check on family connections between staff members, especially if this involves situations where a family connection is acting in a position of responsibility. A classic example of a fraud involving a manager in which family ties were prevalent was Weavering Capital.

Weavering Capital

In brief:

- This was a Macro Fixed Income Fund totalling $640 million in **assets under management (AUM)** as at March 2009.

- The founder and CEO of London-based Weavering Capital was Magnus Peterson.

- In March 2009, the Director, Chas Dabhid, of Weavering Capital alerted the **auditor** of the fund, Ernst & Young, that the assets of Weavering's Macro Fixed Income Fund were 99.98 per cent invested in one derivative instrument.

- The counterparty of the derivative instrument was a British Virgin Islands company called 'Weavering Capital Fund Ltd' which was fully owned and controlled by Magnus Peterson.

- The swaps derivative instrument was first invested into by the fund in 2007, and the position grew throughout 2008 and 2009, in order to counterbalance losses on other investments.

- PricewaterhouseCoopers (PwC) was appointed to liquidate the fund.

Weavering Capital was a London-based manager set up in 1998 by Magnus Peterson, the former Global Head of Proprietary Trading at the Swedish bank SEB in London. Peterson was joined by his wife Amanda, whom he had met whilst working at SEB, and by Chief Economist James Stewart, a PhD economist from the University of Edinburgh and widely quoted on television and in print.

As the company gained authorisation to start business in 1998, the blow up of Long Term Capital Management (LTCM) had caused investors to shy away from the fund market. In 2000, Weavering Capital finally launched its first fund which was relatively small at $50 million AUM but showed good returns from inception. In the first 10 months of trading (March to December 2000) the fund posted amazing returns of 139.6 per cent. In 2001 things soured; by March 2001 the fund had lost 15.06 per cent, and 16.53 per cent the following month. A further collapse of 47.03 per cent in **NAV** in June caused Weavering Capital to close its first fund.

Weavering Capital then launched a Macro Fixed Income Fund in August 2003. The fund was domiciled in the Cayman Islands and listed on the Irish Stock Exchange. In its first few years the fund provided steady returns with Weavering Capital boasting that each year the fund had delivered positive returns, the highest being 11.26 per cent in 2004. Weavering Capital also claimed that in 36 out of 47 months the fund had positive returns. Many investors were drawn to the fund based on its 'proven' track record. The fund was also viewed as a safe investment because of the types of assets it held.

The fund's main investment strategy was supposed to involve trade based on changes in global macroeconomic events. The portfolio was apparently diversified into a variety of fixed income markets, from G7 government bonds through to money market instruments, and the use of derivatives, primarily futures and options. Weavering Capital claimed that its focus was on exploiting opportunities in global interest rate movements. The economic research team, led by James Stewart, would study changes in global interest rates and report their findings to Magnus Peterson, who would then trade based on the information provided.

In November 2008, as the financial crisis was evolving, many investors sought to withdraw their money from 'liquid and safe' funds including Weavering. Weavering quickly received redemption requests totalling $223 million but could only satisfy about $90 million of that. Then, in early March 2009 the company published a note on its website stating that it was 'urgently' investigating the fund's position in a trade. During the same month, Weavering had to call in the liquidators to shut down the fund.

As the liquidators investigated, they found evidence of fraud. The liquidators found that as the fund experienced losses, it did not disclose them to investors, but tried to make up for them by hiding losing positions in other trades. Upon further investigation, the liquidators found that the totality of the fund's $637 million of assets was exposed to a series of interest rate swaps. The swaps' counterparty was a company located in the British Virgin Islands named Weavering Capital Fund Ltd. The heads of the company based in the British Virgin Islands were Magnus Peterson's brother and his stepfather. Effectively Weavering Capital was trying to conceal the fact that it had made massive losses, using a fake interest rate swap traded with a company controlled in essence by the Peterson family.

Investors did not receive their money back. The liquidators tried to collect all that was left but 'only a handful of millions were left instead of hundreds of millions'. In May of 2009 Magnus Peterson was arrested along with one other unidentified man. $475 million is being claimed against Peterson and all of his assets were frozen at the time of his arrest.

The UK's Serious Fraud Office (SFO) pursued an investigation into the collapse of Weavering Capital, but in September 2011 it dropped its investigation citing insufficient evidence to make a prosecution and leaving investors nursing losses of over $500 million. In October 2011 however, the liquidators of Weavering Capital (UK) began a civil lawsuit against Peterson and other previous employees, including his wife, in London's High Court. Peterson is being sued for fraud and breach of his fiduciary duty as director as well as negligence.[1] The case continues.

Lessons learned

1 Be wary of strong control by family members.

- Peterson's family was far too involved with the operations of Weavering companies.

- The **board of directors** included Magnus Peterson (48.67 per cent ownership) and his wife Amanda Peterson (7.08 per cent).

- Peterson's stepfather and brother were directors of the British Virgin Islands fund, revealed as the counterparty to the trades.

2 Note when the investment strategy of the fund stated in the Prospectus is not aligned to current disclosed strategy.

- The initial objectives of the Weavering fund did not match annualised returns and volatility, indicating an obvious misalignment between strategy and reality.

- Volatility measures were divergent to the type of strategy sold under the fund's name.

- Weavering said that the fund's prospectus (which stated that 'no more than 400 per cent of the NAV of the fund may be borrowed by the fund') was 'not relevant to the strategy'. Indeed, on closer analysis the leverage did not match.

---

[1] http://www.ft.com/cms/s/0/1699c72c-f8c7-11e0-ad8f-00144feab49a.html#axzz1mLrJy7IM

It is wise to look into the past history of the company.

■ The first fund that Weavering Capital set up had very volatile returns and was forced to close down.

■ Investors should have drawn their own conclusions with regards to risk associated with any new endeavours by the same team.

3 Check the roles of independent service providers.

■ The Weavering fund's relationship with two futures clearers (ADM Investor Service and Man Financial Group) was not what you would have expected for a fund trading global fixed income.

■ The custodian and administrator of the fund were the same entity (PFPC), which is not usual for the type of strategy Weavering carried out, where money is often held by a **prime broker**.

4 Get information on the manager's corporate governance and systems and controls.

■ Weavering Capital's due diligence questionnaire was only 10 pages long and left many questions unanswered by omission.

■ Cash positioning was subject to weak control.

■ The COO of the firm was also the marketing manager: two roles that I believe are not compatible.

Directors' independence

Funds, as I discussed previously, are often structured as a normal company and therefore will have a board of directors with similar obligations to those of any other directors subject to the jurisdiction of incorporation, for example in the Cayman Islands. Investors should understand who is on the board of the fund to ensure adequate independence as well as skills and integrity. This is particularly true for funds that sit outside of the traditional mutual funds centres.

The relevance of the board of the fund in offshore centres is far less than you might expect. The concept that a fund's board will be freely constituted with the best people, for example, is false since for very simple tax reasons the board of most funds must usually exclude natives from the country where the manager is based. This is another misunderstood conundrum in the industry because it is so different from the traditional fund structures of mutual funds. Investors would expect the board of the fund to be made up of the people they may have met in London or Geneva, but this is prohibited to some extent for example by UK or Swiss tax law. The very basic rule is that a board that is controlled by people in one country could bring that fund into the taxation net of that country. These rules vary country to country and the simple fact of a board having some people from, for example, the UK, does not in itself make the fund a UK taxable company, but it is taken sufficiently seriously for most funds to keep only a minority of directors from the UK. Therefore, following their tax advisors' advice, managers that are usually responsible for the set up of the fund tend to appoint directors who are not resident in the manager's country of origin. This means either appointing people they already know who are willing to take on this role, or specialised professionals. Professional firms usually act individually or as corporate directors and often people related to the administrator will also take on board appointments. A minority of the board will usually include people from the manager.

This leaves plenty of inconsistencies with regards to the impact this type of board will have for an investor in a fund. Will the directors actually have time to properly manage the board? Will a corporate board member provide the right kind of guidance and care? Does the board actually take any decisions independently of the manager?

There are certainly a lot of issues concerning the boards of funds, whether they are related to conflicts of interest, unaccountability to investors, complacency or mere incompetence. A board that would be ideal may include more representatives of the manager but then, in most cases, that causes a tax risk for the fund as I have noted. A board that has professionals who are presumed independent may be, in principle, better, but some of those professionals hold hundreds of directorships and it is unclear what they actually have the capacity to do. Board members from administrators may also face similar issues while they at least have a stake in the business doing well, although that creates another conflict of interest! Similarly, the board members from the manager are all conflicted since it is in their interest for the fund to have as much money under management as possible with the highest NAV. Those who know the fund's strategy best should be ideal candidates, as long as they can be controlled to avoid the abuses seen in recent years. The other obvious truth is that whoever the other board members are they are in reality the appointees of the manager and therefore in many cases have no independence as you hardly ever bite the hand that feeds you!

At present, in my view, there is no perfect board, because the tax situation does not help and because ultimately the funds are not truly independent of the managers, even if, by way of company and fiscal law, they must be. The only solution for investors is to check that the board acts with sufficient integrity so that it will at least offer a cushion of comfort should things go bad. One of the ways to check that there is sufficient integrity is to ensure that there are enough checks and controls and a proper corporate governance culture. To establish this, I know only one way and that is to request relevant board minutes. This at least will give you some insight as to which decisions are properly taken by the board, using what kind of information and under what circumstances. You could also see if there is a proper review by the board of certain important decisions, or of investment management strategy developments, as this indicates that topics are being talked about and reviewed.

A relevant example of where directors failed to do proper reviews on the manager's decisions is Weavering Capital. Further to what I told you about Weavering Capital above, in August 2011 the press reported that Stefan Peterson and Hans Ekstrom, two directors of the Weavering Macro Fixed Income Fund, were found guilty of wilful negligence or default in the exercise of their duties. Each of the directors was fined $111 million for their role in the collapse of the fund as the court found amongst other things that they had signed documents that were put in front of them by the manager 'without applying their minds to their content'. Further, the judge noted that these directors 'never once, in six years, asked any of those they were supposedly supervising to give them a written report or attend a board meeting to provide them with an oral report'.

As we saw during the financial crisis, some boards will rarely review the decisions they are asked to take by the manager even if these decisions are not in the best interest of investors. Of course, they will purport to do so, and may even go through the motions, but the fact is that many board members are either not paid or paid very little for their appointment and view the role as a partial occupation rather than a full-time job. In practice the lack of remuneration does not encourage board members to spend enough time on their job of reviewing and supervising the activities of the service providers of the fund, including the manager. Having said that, regardless of pay, board members actually have fiduciary duties which should compel them to act properly. For investors to have any form of recourse against directors has always been expensive, notably in legal fees, and difficult to do. Even more demoralising for investors the framework usually allows directors to pay for their legal costs from the assets of the fund (thus the investor will end up paying two sets of legal fees).

Proper boards do of course exist, and professional independent individuals will help remove conflicts of interest and provide more credibility to board decisions, especially in times of difficulty. This is more and more the case in Europe under the **UCITS** format which could easily be exported to other parts of the world. In the meantime a review of the backgrounds of the fund directors remains a crucial part of determining a fund's legal and ethical integrity as well as compliance with relevant rules and regulations, and I highly recommend it.

Management dedication

When an asset manager is telling you how good their performance is, it is legitimate that you know how much of their time is dedicated to managing the relevant fund. It is very time consuming to be a great money manager. Due to the psychological emotions alone, not to mention the time you should be watching the markets, reading research or talking to market players, it is a full-time job. If a manager has time for anything else, including to talk to you or other investors too often, you have to ask yourself what their dedication to looking after their fund is. This is a small but pertinent question. In my view, had Madoff been behind computer screens all day he might have been more credible as an asset manager (see Chapter 1 for the Madoff case study). Playing golf does not usually form part of the life of a person focusing on asset management, at least not in my book, and is not compatible with good governance. An asset manager spending his time on operations or on marketing again does not reflect well. These absences are all warning signs and in fact if someone else is responsible for managing the money then find out about them!

Some managers also sometimes delegate more than one strategy or different financial products to one asset manager. This is almost always an issue as a momentary lapse of concentration could cost an investment strategy very dearly. It is useful, therefore, to find out about commitments and ask the right questions about what other strategies might require in terms of time and/or concentration and if they are sufficiently related to the main strategy too.

Summary

- Corporate governance involves understanding if the individuals controlling your money are organised around a reliable framework that is of a high standing.

- Find out who the main people involved are including the directors and the investment management team.

- The manager should have staff in different departments with specific roles and responsibilities.

- Ensure the adequate independence, skills and integrity of directors.

- Assess how committed the manager is to looking after your money.

5

Service providers

What topics are covered in this chapter?

- The missing link – the investor
- Administrator
- Prime broker and custodian
- Other key providers

To understand the risks of a **fund**, it is vital to understand who the relevant service providers are and the terms of their engagement by the fund. This will offer valuable insights into the reliability of a fund and how well it is serviced by specialists. Just as no investor would want to invest in a fund using a **manager** who is viewed as incompetent, so no investor should want to invest in a fund with poor administration or banking services. Service providers are the backbone of a fund's outsourced operations and their ability to carry out their duties should be assessed as much as any other aspect of the fund.

The missing link – the investor

Service providers offer different packages of services to funds and there is a vast array of service providers available, each of varying quality, but most notably each offering contracts that are more or less complete in terms of investor protection. This means that funds can enter into a contract with a service provider and accept the service provider's standard terms and conditions without reviewing whether such terms are in the investors' favour. The contract that binds the fund to the service provider is not one to which you, as investor, are a party, and generally investors hardly think to ask to see it. Unfortunately it is usually heavily weighted in favour of the service provider: the investor is simply left out of the loop.

As we saw during the financial crisis, frauds and failures have happened where reputable companies were servicing funds. To date, few if any service providers have been held responsible for the losses suffered by investors. This is because they are protected by the provisions of biased contractual terms. This is another reason why due diligence is very important as you can only rely on what you know, not what you are told or on any impression you may have when you see a famous name linked to a fund! If you don't believe me just consider Lehman or Refco (see Chapter 8): two big names that went down taking a lot of investors' money with them. Any impression of safety from working with these well established companies was deluded. Similarly, the Madoff (see Chapter 1) or Weavering funds (see Chapter 5) benefited from top-rank servicing companies and yet they allegedly missed the underlying fraud and did not protect investors.

Let me illustrate the point more clearly with three Madoff related Luxembourg and Ireland based funds, the Luxalpha Sicav Fund (also discussed in Chapter 1), the Herald (Lux) US Absolute Return Fund and the Thema International Fund.

---

case study   **Madoff funds and high-quality service providers**

Luxalpha Sicav

In brief:

■ Luxalpha Sicav was a Luxembourg **UCITS** fund launched in February 2004.

■ The fund boasted famous service providers such as UBS (Luxembourg) S.A. that acted as its **custodian** and **administrator**, and Ernst & Young as the **auditors** of the fund.

▶

The fund was linked to Madoff's Ponzi scheme (see Chapter 1) and subsequently went into liquidation in April 2009.

■ UBS denied responsibility, refusing to honour redemption requests amounting to €32 million from the fund's shareholders. UBS argued that the fund was created at the request of sophisticated investors who knowingly invested in a fund that was linked to Bernard L. Madoff Investment Securities LLC.

■ In March 2009, investors filed a series of complaints against UBS with the Luxembourg courts, but these were dismissed as inadmissible. The courts ruled that liquidators alone (not shareholders/investors) could seek to recover a fund's capital assets.

■ In December 2009, the fund's liquidator, Irving Picard, launched a series of claims totalling approximately $1.7 billion against UBS and Ernst & Young.

■ These claims have yet to be settled and could take years to be judged, leaving investors without compensation for the time being[1].

Herald (Lux) US Absolute Return Fund

In brief:

■ A Luxembourg-based UCITS fund, Herald (Lux) US Absolute Return Fund, was launched in February 2008.

■ The fund's custodian and administrator was HSBC Securities Services Luxembourg. HSBC employed Bernard L. Madoff Investment Securities LLC to act as sub-custodian of the fund.

■ Similar to the Luxalpha fund above, the Herald fund failed as a result of its link to Madoff and was forced to liquidate its assets in December 2008.

■ In April 2009, for the first time a fund sued its custodian in Luxembourg: the Herald fund sued HSBC for a total of €1.6 billion on the basis that HSBC failed to protect investors' money when it employed Bernard L. Madoff Investment Securities LLC as sub-custodian.

■ The court case is still pending.

Thema International Fund Plc

In brief:

■ Thema International Fund Plc ('Thema fund') was an Irish UCITS fund launched in December 2006.

[1] http://mobile.bloomberg.com/news/2011-11-15/ubs-ernst-young-are-sued-again-by-luxembourg-madoff-funds

Bank Medici AG acted as Thema fund's manager, and HSBC Securities Services (Ireland) Limited and HSBC Institutional Trust Services (Ireland) Limited (HSBC) acted as the fund's custodian and provided administration and other services.

■ Thema fund was a Madoff feeder fund. Shortly after Madoff's Ponzi scheme was discovered the Thema fund suspended redemptions.

■ The manager's (Bank Medici) founder, Sonja Kohn, allegedly assisted Madoff in criminal activities involving Madoff's Ponzi scheme.

■ Investors of the Thema fund filed a group lawsuit against HSBC in January 2009, one month after Madoff's fraud was uncovered. Investors argued that since HSBC provided administrative services to the fund it should have known about the fraud.

■ HSBC estimated that the purported **net asset value** of the Thema fund as at 30 November 2008 was $1.1 billion and that the fund's actual transfers to Madoff Securities minus its actual withdrawals were approximately $312 million.

■ In June 2011, HSBC agreed to pay $62.5 million to settle the lawsuit.[2]

■ However, in September 2011, a Manhattan federal judge rejected HSBC's proposed $62.5 million settlement because the judge deemed the amount to be 'not fair, reasonable or adequate – even at this preliminary stage' for the Thema fund's investors.

■ The judge said he would consider a revised accord.

■ In November 2011, HSBC proposed a revised settlement ranging from $52.5 million to $62.5 million, depending on how many investors choose not to join the accord.[3]

These examples show you that the famous names of service providers are not enough to provide security for your money. To dig even deeper, read an extract of Madoff's interview with the *Financial Times* in April 2011, taken from behind bars in North Carolina. Although

---

[2] http://www.bloomberg.com/news/2011-06-07/hsbc-agrees-to-pay-62.5-million-to-settle-u-s-class-action-madoff-suit.html

[3] http://newsandinsight.thomsonreuters.com/Legal/News/2011/11_-_November/HSBC_proposes_amended_settlement_in_Madoff_case/

> Madoff's word cannot be trusted (as history has shown!), perhaps there is some truth in his warnings about big-name institutions:

> > Madoff is also profoundly cynical about the rest of Wall Street, pointing out that the large banks not only handled his cash, but also marketed his funds. 'UBS and HSBC are going to have big problems – Picard is suing all of these [banks] and he thinks he can get $50bn or so. HSBC sat up there twice and set up and looked over my books and records, for two weeks, and missed things. The big difference between the big banks and funds, and regular clients, is that the banks and funds have all the information from the regulatory filings – but the regular clients did not have. Price Waterhouse came up to my office once a year and checked things out.'

> > UBS says it was not aware of any wrongdoing by Madoff. HSBC says it did not know that fraud was being committed and lost $1bn of its own as a result. HSBC never marketed Madoff funds to its clients, while UBS and other banks did.

> > In Madoff's eyes, JPMorgan is also tarnished by association. Before JPMorgan and Chase Manhattan merged in 2001, Madoff had his accounts with Chase. So did some of his first clients, such as Levy. But the bank never raised alarm bells. 'Look, I am not a banker but I know that billions of dollars going in and out of a bank account is something that should alert you to something. [They] got all the financial statements. [They] could have seen – I was using them as custodian, and they never questioned it,' he insists.[4]

> Some of Madoff's predictions materialised four months later in August 2011 when Irving Picard filed a modified claim against UBS for $2 billion on the basis that UBS was allegedly an accomplice to fraud in its role as custodian of the Luxalpha fund.

Administrator

One of the most important service providers for a fund is the administrator. The principal role of the administrator remains that of accounting and notably providing the **net asset value (NAV)**. The administrator usually takes on various other roles including keeping the shareholders register and acting as paying agent for subscriptions and redemptions.

[4] Gelles, D. and Tett, G. (2011) 'From behind bars, Madoff spins his story', FT Weekend Magazine, 9 April, pp. 14–21.

The independence of the administrator is one of the keys to the legitimacy of the fund. The manager is also paid based on the NAV and therefore it is imperative that the NAV is properly and independently established.

Valuation of hard-to-value assets

It is sometimes very hard, even for specialists, to value assets. The valuation of assets is generally taken at market price, book value or according to best practice. When there is no market price, such as is often the case with hard-to-value assets, the administrator faces immediate difficulties, as it would not normally have the expertise or tools to assess the value of such assets. Therefore, it is common if not always the case that as a matter of contract and thus practice, service providers tend to rely on the manager's prices, which is not always in the investors' best interest.

Accounting rules for the valuation of assets

Assets are usually valued according to three levels:

- *level 1* – liquid assets, such as exchange traded instruments;
- *level 2* – assets for which valuation is based on readily available models; and
- *level 3* – illiquid securities for which valuation should be obtained from specialist independent sources (e.g. complex derivatives, private equity investments or diamonds).

Valuation for level 3 types of securities should be obtained from independent experts, however, and this is the biggest problem as it is expensive to arrange. Usually such assets are valued, not by the administrator, but based on the relevant manager's prices using its assumptions and expectations. Sometimes the pricing is also taken from banks (e.g. the ones that acted as brokers or custodians on the sale of such assets). Neither of these two methods provides any comfort for investors as neither is free of conflicts of interest! In fact quite the opposite, since everyone from the manager to the brokers and custodians involved usually gets paid according to the highest level of assets!

The manager's role in valuation

If I were an investor, I would want to understand if a fund invests in assets that are hard to value or illiquid. Hard-to-value assets can cause potential problems in terms of the NAV of the fund because, as already noted, an administrator might not always be sufficiently equipped in terms of market data tools to determine the relevant value of an asset. Sometimes it is also a question of liability, with administrators not wanting to be responsible for quoting the wrong price. As such they agree with the fund and the manager that if the assets are hard to value the administrator can call on the manager, **prime broker** or other brokers for assistance and not be held accountable if the price is wrong. Therefore confirm with the administrator the degree of the manager's involvement and I always urge investors to look into the reasons for a manager's past intervention in asset valuation.

By way of case study of the manager's powers and the limits of the administrator's role, consider the language used in the fictitious **prospectus** of the regulated fund below. You will come across prospectuses that clearly set out the level of involvement of the manager and other parties with regards to pricing the fund's assets. This example prospectus wording is not uncommon. The emphasised words are the ones that investors need to focus on.

> ### Example: Prospectus and price sources from conflicted parties
>
> For the purpose of determining the value of the fund's assets, in the performance of its duties the Administrator *shall rely upon information as provided by pricing sources such as brokers, custodians, prime brokers* or any pricing agencies, and the valuations or statements provided by these pricing sources shall be deemed to be the last available price. *In relation to assets that are not listed, the Administrator may rely on valuations provided by the Investment Manager*, the prime broker or any third party authorised to that effect by the fund.
>
> Valuations or statements of accounts as provided by the pricing sources (i.e. prime brokers, custodians, other brokers or pricing agencies) shall be considered as the most reliable information on which the *Administrator shall carry out no control*. The *Administrator shall not be held liable for any valuation error* due to the pricing sources. Should a valuation error come to the attention of the Administrator, it will liaise with the Investment Manager in order to adjust the valuation.
>
> The *Administrator has no duty of ensuring the accuracy or consistency of the valuations* provided by relevant pricing sources, subject to the preceding paragraph.
>
> The Administrator, having due regard to the standard of care and due diligence in this respect, may, when calculating the NAV, *completely and exclusively rely*, unless there is manifest error on its part, upon the valuations provided either (i) by the *Investment Manager*, (ii) by various pricing sources available on the market such as pricing agencies (i.e. Bloomberg, Reuters) or administrators of underlying funds, (iii) by *prime brokers and brokers*, or (iv) by (a) specialist(s) *duly authorised to that effect by the Investment Manager*.

▶

> In particular, for the ***valuation of any assets for which market quotations or fair market values are not publicly available*** (including but not limited to non-listed structured or credit-related instruments and other illiquid assets), the ***Administrator will exclusively rely on valuations provided either by the Investment Manager*** or by ***third party pricing sources appointed by the Investment Manager*** under its responsibility or other official pricing sources like funds' administrators and others like Telekurs, Bloomberg, Reuters and will not check the correctness and accuracy of the valuations so provided. If the Investment Manager gives instructions to the Administrator to use a specific pricing source, the Investment Manager undertakes to make its own prior due diligence on such agents as far as its competence, reputation, professionalism are concerned so as to ensure that the prices which will be given to the Administrator are reliable and the Administrator will not, and shall not be required to, carry out any additional due diligence or testing on any such pricing source. ***So far as these assets are concerned, the sole responsibility of the Administrator is to compute the NAV on the basis of the prices provided by the Investment Manager*** or the other appointed third party pricing source(s), without any responsibility whatsoever (in the absence of manifest error) on the correctness or accuracy of the valuations provided by the relevant sources. ***For the avoidance of doubt, the Administrator will not effect any testing on valuations on prices nor collect or analyse any supporting documents which will assess or evidence the accuracy of the prices of any asset held in the portfolio*** for which a price or valuation is provided in accordance with the Section 'Suspension/ Deferral of Calculation of NAV, Subscriptions and Redemptions.

Now you may be wondering why you are investing in funds when the NAV may be unreliable. One factor here is historical. When alternative funds first started in the US it was common for them to provide the prices of the assets they held. The abuse of that position of trust by a few managers in recent times has meant that it has become almost taboo for a fund to have its own valuation service. We then saw a move to potentially more reliable professional administrators to calculate the NAV. Regrettably, the supposed third party administrators would still rely largely on the information provided by the manager, without the need to verify the accuracy of that information. Clearly there is a conflict in this situation which can only be controlled if proper checks and balances are performed by the parties involved. Provided that such controls are in place, it should not be seen as unreasonable for an administrator to rely on the manager as a valuable source of information for valuation. The reality, however, is that often the administrator 'shall carry out no control' and has 'no duty of ensuring the accuracy and/or consistency of the valuations' as noted in the above example. Thus the frauds continue to occur even when you have famous service providers, which are not responsible!

This problem will continue and is quite shocking. Even recent legislation has not sought to address this head on. Nothing short of improving the responsibilities of the administrator will diminish the risk of abuse or fraud. Further, a new approach needs to be taken when it comes to sourcing prices for hard-to-value assets, such as insisting on using a group of pre-approved independent specialists. Such an approach would have avoided Madoff and plenty of lesser scandals that nonetheless proved ruinous for investors who believed that the administration of funds was operated with more independence. Not much has changed as I write this book, regardless of new laws brought about by various governments in Europe and the US.

Is there true independent administration?

After the failures of 2008 and post-Madoff the pressure has grown to appoint independent administrators. An independent administrator should give an impartial and accurate valuation of the fund's assets so that investors are paying the appropriate fees and can feel comfortable that the overall value of the fund is reliable. It is ironic that the appointment of independent administrators has come about after Madoff because Madoff never had a fund as such (the funds managed belonged to other people with administration services!) and accordingly Madoff would never have had use for an administrator. Nevertheless, since then a number of larger funds, such as DE Shaw Group and Elliott Management, have made the move away from self-administration and towards independent administration. As you can guess from what I have said, this is only part of the solution … obviously there should be more independence but we are still surrounded by issues of pricing difficulties and conflicts.

Even if a fund has an independent administrator this does not preclude the possibility that it could be involved in fraudulent activities. For example, when Weavering Capital failed, a lot of scrutiny went into why a fund with a long-standing reputation and a well-regarded UK-based administrator, PFPC International Ltd, had suddenly been found out to be a fraud. As discussed in Chapter 4, Weavering, which was set up in 1998, went into liquidation following redemption requests that could not be honoured. The fund had been valued at $506 million. Yet according to the liquidator, PricewaterhouseCoopers (PwC), once it investigated Weavering's books it discovered that the Weavering Macro Fixed Income fund's only major asset was a $637 million 'interest rate swap'. Further, PwC said that this derivatives contract 'had been struck with a company which was revealed to be related to the manager [which] lacked the value necessary to support the swaps.'[5] This is a typical case of what can go wrong in the alternative industry and it happened whilst UK regulated companies were involved.

The agreement between the fund and the administrator

Often agreements between administrators and funds leave neither party accountable for the accuracy of valuations. Whilst there are many worthwhile discussions that surround the issues of liability, common sense denotes that an accountant whose purpose is to account for the holdings of a company/fund should be more accountable regarding asset valuation. Unfortunately this is not the case, essentially because of contracts that are crafted to avoid any blame or responsibility regardless of the quality of the accounting job. It seems that through disclaimers and limitation of liability clauses, many professionals avoid any responsibility for the tasks they are charged to perform whilst on the face of it they are presented to the investor as being fully responsible and accountable for that role. The bottom line is that the legal system, and notably contract law, is used to protect some fund professionals from their actual responsibilities, mostly unbeknown to investors, who are not blameless but who do not think to read the relevant contracts, since they are not a party to them. Even if they read such contracts and meant to seek amendments they would not have the influence or the means to cause any changes to be made. This is a major stigma in the financial industry. To date this situation has not been grasped by politicians or lobbyists and is not, therefore, improving.

In the end what this means is that rather than trusting a well-known administrator's name printed on a prospectus and marketing materials, investors should look at the actual contract between the administrator and the fund for specific areas of responsibility. The majority of such contracts, and all the ones I have seen, still allow the

---

[5] http://www.guardian.co.uk/business/2009/mar/20/weavering-hedge-fund-liquidation

administrator to source valuation for positions from managers or relevant brokers, all of which are conflicted, without performing proper checks on the same.

The contract should be checked to see who is responsible and liable for valuation, what the cost of the administrator is (try to determine whether the manager negotiated well on behalf of the fund and what those costs cover) and who is responsible for checking investors against anti-money laundering rules.

Example: Contractual responsibilities of an administrator

Consider this example of an administration agreement on which I worked that sets out specific areas of responsibility and explicitly stated that the **valuation agent** (defined below) could rely on the manager's/**advisor**'s pricing quotations.

Snapshot of a middle/back office service agreement

> The Valuation Agent (in charge of providing middle/back office support as well as valuation services to the fund) ... relies on the manager's/advisor's pricing procedures.

The same fund's prospectus in light of this contract noted that:

> ... in relation to the NAV, unless pricing is publicly available, it is the responsibility of the directors to determine in good faith the pricing to be used, including potentially querying the advisor and manager with regard to the relevant pricing used.

In order to effectively ensure that the manager does not manipulate or influence the valuation of assets, the contract with the administrator must be more carefully prepared. Perhaps a way to appease investors' concerns about the reliability of fund asset valuations is through the adoption of a standardised fund valuation agreement, as noted in my comment below made in the *Financial Times* back in April 2008. I argue that a binding master agreement, clearly setting out a reliable approach to asset valuation and introducing legal liability for managers and administrators, should be implemented across the investment industry. Such an agreement would certainly increase investor confidence, protect the industry's reputation and avoid political interference:

Valuation problems need in-house solution

Talking Head

Jérôme de Lavenére Lussan

The way hedge fund assets are valued gives real cause for concern and there appears to be no solution in sight.

The problem is not a new one, and various bodies have put forward ideas on how the industry could improve, including the Financial Services Authority, the Hedge Funds Working Group and the Association of Alternative Investment Managers.

But funds continue to blow up as a result of inadequate valuation techniques, threatening the stability of markets and the hedge fund industry. The surprising failure by either regulators or market participants to tackle such a prominent issue may reflect vested interests against change.

Whatever the reasons, this is a risk for the development of the industry and has opened the door to political interventionism, to the possible detriment of the freedom that has made the hedge fund industry a major contributor to market efficiencies.

The valuation of assets is key to investor confidence and the continued growth of the hedge fund industry. Valuation issues and the fear of 'fund blow ups' will therefore, quite rightly, be at the forefront of regulators' and investors' minds.

The industry needs to accept a form of practice that is adopted by all and acceptable internationally. This should limit complicated regulations and still afford some freedom for specialised hedge fund managers.

Some of the problems with valuation are simple to deal with. For example, the concept of independence should be paramount and any fund still valuing its own assets should be highlighted to investors as a potentially riskier investment with a standard form of 'health warning'. This approach may not suit those who prefer to see only independent third party valuation but it would allow investors to choose their funds accordingly.

The other simple problem is to agree the way valuation should be effected by any asset valuer. This is relevant for hard-to-value assets that have again caused concerns recently, with the credit squeeze showing obvious valuation problems – even with the most reputable companies.

The only way to give the market confidence in the valuation processes is for the processes to be of a recognised international standard. Funds and third party valuers adopting the standard would state that and gain from it. Processes may be more difficult to agree, but there are already good drafts of general principles available.

Funds not abiding by such processes would stand out as non-compliant and again investors would be able to choose accordingly. Institutional investors would be under pressure to invest in funds with appropriate processes and thus the industry would protect itself naturally.

These two approaches would at least rid us of the problem of independence and valuation techniques and allow the industry to focus on much more complex problems.

If we know the industry has suffered from valuation problems, even with the very best companies, we ought to recognise that something else is at work that is limiting the quality of the valuation work done. Conflicts of interest are one problem. Managers clearly benefit from higher valuations and service providers benefit from richer managers. The other flaw is that no one wants to be responsible for the valuation of hard-to-value assets where errors could leave the valuers facing huge liabilities.

Finally, there is little if any independent monitoring of the independent asset valuers. Even the most sophisticated investors can get it wrong and invest in assets that were poorly valued, despite having carried out due diligence on valuation techniques. There are other problems that lead to certain valuation anomalies but they are less important, such as the smoothing out of valuations on a month by month basis to reduce volatility.

one way of dealing with all three problems identified above is to suggest a standardised contract for funds, managers and valuers, as banks have done when dealing with the ISDA master agreement of the International Swaps and Derivative Association. This approach would encourage the parties to take responsibility within agreed limits, and reduce the potential for accusations of negligence.

It would also allow valuers to remain independent when looking to value a hard-to-value asset.

These provisions are particularly commendable because of the obvious conflicts of interest that arise when the investment managers or prime brokers are consulted at a time when independence is most needed.

Jérôme de Lavenére Lussan is managing partner at Laven Partners

Source: Financial Times, 21 January 2008

Figure 5.1

Other checks to perform on administrators

Moving away from these fundamental problems, there are some other business aspects that you can scrutinise when evaluating the fund's use of an administrator, for example the time taken by the administrator to produce the NAV. Some investors find that certain administrators take too much time to produce their valuations. You can easily check how quickly NAV is produced after the relevant period and the more delays the more you should be concerned. Delays could indicate that there is a high volume of hard-to-value assets in the fund's portfolio or could even be a sign of incompetence; in either case you need to check out why there are delays.

Other insightful information could be found through asking questions about the length of time taken to confirm the NAV, and whether the NAV has ever had to be restated or delayed. If so, you need to be told the reasons behind this and decide if further concerns emerge from such explanations. Delays or changes in NAV reporting could be potential indications of weaknesses in the valuation process.

You could also review the administrator's experience in relation to the relevant asset class. Even more generally investors should know how long the administrator has been in business, the amount of clients it provides NAVs for, the strategies of the clients it covers and the services in addition to the calculation of the NAV that it provides. Another simple question to ask is how long the administrator has been providing services for the fund. If the fund has recently changed administrator, further investigation might be necessary to determine the nature and reasons for the change.

Asset valuation is, in my view, the most important role of the administrator and needs to be examined thoroughly during any review of your potential fund. The administrator should be asked what sources it uses to get pricing information and how frequently it sources information from the prime broker, brokers, custodian or manager. Careful due diligence should go into the valuation process as soon as the assets are less liquid or hard to value. The administrator should explain if it has an operating memorandum and what information it uses to value the fund's assets.

At the end what counts is determining if the administrator independently values assets using outside sources, effects the valuation using some information provided by the manager, or if it simply confirms valuations made by the manager or quotes from broker statements. The manager should ideally have as small a role as possible when it comes to dealing with the NAV of the fund to avoid conflicts of interest.

Prime broker and custodian

A bank normally services a fund with regards to the safekeeping of its assets. This role is called a custodian but can also be linked to the role of prime broker. The service is an essential one to the fund management industry. Prime brokers provide services mostly to alternative funds but also to normal funds and regulated funds trading all forms of derivatives or shorting stocks. The role of the prime broker probably needs to be understood better. Not all alternative funds will have a prime broker. A fund largely invested in private companies for example will not need the services of a prime broker just as a fund investing in wines or art does not need a prime broker either and neither do those trading futures such as **CTAs**. Funds that readily use prime brokers are those dealing with certain types of instruments that are provided by a large bank or those that need to short stocks. The prime broker is mostly a term used for the bank that services any fund that deals in publicly quoted stocks and needs to borrow such stocks for shorting purposes or needs associated credit lines for leverage purposes. The prime broker generally also gathers all trades from other brokers, thus the name prime broker. It is now a generic term that applies as easily to traditional strategies that require some lending as to CTA clearing houses.

Understanding the underlying purpose and role of any relevant bank is key, as was demonstrated in 2008 when banks were potentially going bust.

Check which bank is acting for the fund

First things first, get to know if the prime broker or custodian is truly acting for the fund. Some funds have lied about this. It is quite acceptable to seek written confirmation from the bank directly that it was, and still is, appointed in this capacity. You should also establish, where relevant, how many prime brokers the fund deals with. This is called 'multiple prime' and is encouraged since the default of larger prime brokers during the financial crisis. Note that the idea of having more than one prime broker is sort of a misnomer since, as we discussed above, a prime broker is for all intents and purposes a role for just one aggregator of trades. Normally the use of two prime brokers upsets prime brokers themselves as in reality one makes more money than the other by servicing the main needs of the fund, whilst the other is more or less on standby where notably cash is held in reserves to avoid loss of money in the case of the insolvency of the other main prime broker. Funds usually divide the cash assets across such prime brokers. If the fund uses several prime brokers, more controls will have to be exercised by the manager so that all order management is properly followed and risks of losses including from a defaulting counterparty are limited.

Where the prime broker is small in terms of value or business size, a check should be run on the prime brokerage firm to ensure that they don't have any pending lawsuits against them. This reveals something about their quality of service and may also indicate a future financial problem if the value of potential claims is high, which could expose the assets of the clients of the prime broker to a potential insolvency. In practice most regulators will have some form of publicly accessible records to check this.

Whilst many regulators do not produce a list of registered prime brokers per se, you can nonetheless research individual brokers or brokerage firms on the relevant regulator's website. For example, you could search the name of a UK-based prime broker on the FSA Register. In the US, the Financial Industry Regulatory Authority (FINRA) has a very useful free tool that allows investors to search the professional backgrounds of current and former FINRA-registered brokerage firms and brokers: the FINRA BrokerCheck.

For a list of prime brokers you could also do a simple Google search or take a look at, for example, the prime brokerage guide website: **www. primebrokerageguide.com**. Although such lists are informative, it is always best to check the official regulator's website to ensure that the prime broker is currently registered and has a clean track record.

Experience and reporting systems

Another useful check should be in connection with the prime broker's experience. Like the administrator, the prime broker should have some expertise with the specialised assets of the fund so that transactions can be processed smoothly. It is surprising how many brokers are operating using old information systems, which causes confusion on trade reports and errors. Where possible, if you have access to the prime broker statements, you can almost immediately deduce the level of quality. This is mostly relevant to smaller houses.

There is a connection between low-quality services and the performance of the fund. Because the relationship with the prime broker is handled by the manager even if the prime broker services the fund, the more difficulty a manager has working with the bank of the fund, the more time a manager is likely to spend on operations, or to face trade errors. All of this is not usually good for the fund's performance.

Using an independent bank

As a constant warning, even if a fund has an independent prime broker this does not preclude the possibility that it could be involved in fraudulent activities. This is nothing new and a good service provider does not prevent an even better fraudster from abusing investors!

Consider the example of MF Global (previously known as Man Financial Services), a US registered brokerage firm, which faced allegations of fraud following the collapse of the $230 million Philadelphia Alternative Asset Management (PAAM) hedge fund.

---

case study   **MF Global**

In brief:

■ In June 2005, PAAM hedge fund was charged with fraud by the **Commodity Futures Trading Commission (CFTC)** for allegedly stealing from investors and concealing trading losses of $140 million.

■ In 2007, MF Global was charged a total of $77 million to settle claims with US regulators over allegations that it played a part in hiding PAAM's manager's fraudulent actions.

■ One of MF Global's top executives, Thomas Gilmartin, was also fined $250,000 by the CFTC for his handling of PAAM's accounts.

■ The CFTC said that both MF Global and Gilmartin 'failed to diligently supervise the handling of the **offshore** fund accounts (of PAAM) … and failed to respond to indications of questionable activity'.

Affiliated brokers and custodians

It is insightful to investigate whether any of the brokers are affiliated to the manager. This is such a source of conflict that such a relationship should be avoided. This was one of the issues in the Madoff case of course, but even outside this extreme example, the fact that a fund might be working with an affiliated broker just opens up too many issues of conflict to be really worthwhile. Like the administrator, the fund's brokers should be as independent as possible. If there is a questionable connection between the fund and the broker, more due diligence may be necessary to make sure that the broker's gains are not covering for the fund's losses. A legitimate fund will usually have a legitimate prime broker.

Cash protection

The fund needs to protect its cash using a good bank. Cash is harder to protect as usually it gets mixed up with other assets of the prime broker or custodian. This is also true of securities but if the securities are in the name of the fund there is a good chance the fund will have a solid claim over them. You should therefore review, if possible, how the prime broker or custodian proposes to manage cash assets and its policies on segregation. Most funds have some cash with prime brokers or other custodians that is not invested so check how this cash is handled. Ideally any cash should be put into separate accounts from the rest of the fund's assets and segregated from the assets of other clients of the prime broker or custodian.

See the section on back office workflow in Chapter 6 for further detailed explanation on cash protection.

The agreement between the prime broker/custodian and the fund

Finally, the contract between the prime broker and the fund should be carefully examined. There is also usually a contract between the fund and a custodian but this is not always the case as traditionally parties have relied on their own practices to cover their actions. In any case the contract should specify the amount the fund pays to the bank for its services. The contract might also have provisions regarding certain trading thresholds. Importantly the contract for prime brokers should stipulate the kind of assets the prime broker will trade for the fund and its accessibility to any non-traditional assets. In addition all contracts should set out rules on the segregation of assets, which are often complex and can be drafted in ways that sometimes lack clarity.

Other key providers

Legal advisors

Traditionally the market tends to rely on the **legal advisor** for quality and that is absolutely fine. In my view all members of the Bar should work to the same standard, just like doctors would in their own professional way. For legal work, especially in Europe and notably the UK we have seen a trend since the eighties towards favouring larger firms which may not necessarily be a good thing. Indeed the underlying issue lies with the fact that there is confusion as to who the lawyers are acting for – and it is never for investors! Let me repeat this, the law firm, the name of which you have placed your trust upon, does *not* act for you. This is also very clearly stated in the prospectus. So this point is worth bearing in mind when investing. Ultimately, in private equity funds for example, investors will ask their own lawyers to review relevant fund documents. This is hardly ever done in the case of funds. This leaves the investors much at the mercy of the fund's lawyers. Presumably the better they are, the harsher the prospectus.

Auditor

The auditor is another crucial service provider. To some extent this is a tremendously important aspect of the industry as a lot of reliance is placed on the auditor notably in relation to the audit of the fund's financial statements. However, as we have seen through recent frauds, auditors are not always able to provide the necessary protections for investors. This failure in the profession is an issue linked to many complexities, one of which is that the audit work is not simple, but nor is it necessarily highly paid. In the end this means that checks are not made on information provided by funds and/or managers. If any information is misleading, this can have grave consequences for the investor. For many investors this should mean that regardless of the named auditor they should themselves review financial statements as part of their due diligence ahead of making an investment. For the small and mid-size investor this is hard to do, but it is the best way to see what the fund carried in its books. If you do not have such expertise or resources then start by considering the checks below. These searches would be all the more relevant if you do not recognise the name of the auditor. Many small audit firms have excellent credentials, but we are in a world where the abuse of a few has given many perfectly professional practitioners a bad name. Having said that, well-known auditors are also quite capable of making mistakes ... and of failing to spot frauds.

The checks you can carry out include ensuring that the auditor is independent. A large client (a large fund) using a small auditor should be viewed as suspicious as this potentially leaves the fund with the capacity to unduly influence the auditor. Indeed the revenues derived by the auditor from such a large client could make up a significant portion of the auditor's overall profits and you can see where that might lead. A general search can be run on the auditing firm for example to determine if there are any publicly available records of legal proceedings against them.

The auditor can also be asked more passive questions about its relationship with the fund, for example the last time the fund was audited, the frequency of the audits and their scope. This helps work out whether the representations made by the manager are also true! As the case of Seaside Asset Management showed, some people are quite capable of using the name of an auditor whilst the auditor may not actually be involved in the work claimed. In this example it was reported in April 2010 that Habif, Arogeti & Wynne, an Atlanta accounting firm, which compiled unaudited financial data and prepared annual tax returns for Seaside Asset Management's fund had sought a temporary restraining order to bar Seaside Asset Management from using its name. The accountancy firm claims that the fund used its name to confuse investors into believing that they were the official auditor of Seaside.

A classic example of when investors should have reviewed the service provider, specifically the auditor of the fund, is the Bayou Fund.

---

case study   # Bayou Fund

In brief:

- Bayou Hedge Fund Group was founded in 1996 by Samuel Israel III (CEO).

- Bayou raised approximately $400 million from investors.

- Between 1997 and 2002 investors were defrauded as funds were misappropriated for personal use.

- In 1998 investors were lied to about the fund's poor returns and a fictitious accounting firm, Richmond-Fairfield Associates, was set up to provide misleading audited results.

- In 2004 Israel and Daniel Marino (CFO) stopped trading and transferred the rest of Bayou's assets to Israel and other non-Bayou entities. Meanwhile, Bayou still sent statements to investors indicating profitable trades.

- In 2005 the SEC filed an enquiry into Bayou; and Israel and Marino pleaded guilty to multiple charges including conspiracy and fraud.

- Israel was sentenced to 22 years in prison in 2008.

- Israel faked his own suicide on 10 June 2008, the day he was supposed to start his prison sentence, but he turned himself in to the Massachusetts authorities a few weeks later.

Lessons learned

- Verification of service providers – it would have been useful to do a check on Bayou's accounting firm.

- The manager's work history and civil or criminal record – a **background check** would have shown that Israel had lied to investors about his previous work experience and also had a criminal record.

Summary

▓ Service providers are the backbone of a fund's outsourced operations.

▓ There is a vast array of service providers of varying quality.

▓ Even famous big name service providers may not be enough to provide security for your money.

▓ Types of service providers include:
  - Administrator – one of the most important service providers as it calculates the NAV.
  - Custodian – normally a bank, holds the fund's assets.
  - Prime broker – provides securities lending and leveraged trade execution.
  - Legal advisors – provide legal advice to the fund.
  - Auditors – audit the fund's financial statements.

▓ Check the agreement between the fund and each service provider – who is liable for what and is the service provider independent?

6

Front and back office operations

What topics are covered in this chapter?

- Internal operational policies
- Verifying the application of policies
- Front office workflow
- Back office workflow
- The future balance of power between front and back office

In this chapter I will cover the work flow that is vital for management strategies and the functions that link the asset managers and notably traders in the front office to the back office staff. I cannot stress enough how important it is to understand fully the front to back office operations of the **manager**, as this is where you will find the weaknesses that always seem to be part of the frauds or failures we have seen in the industry. Although it may take an expert to understand some of the operations and to set them up properly, it takes no genius to spot the weaknesses that are relevant. Mostly, it just takes time.

Internal operational policies

The first thing to do is to ensure that the manager's operational policies and procedures are well documented, well executed and enforced internally. As with many things in finance, the term 'operations' has no set definition, but it is often understood to mean front and back office only. Thus, 'operations' implies the trading systems that allow for the generation of orders, their record keeping and their transfer to an independent person in the same company who assesses whether those trades have been properly executed by the underlying broker who received the orders. To review operations more fully however, one must consider and assess the main people responsible including the Chief Operating Officer (COO) and/or the Chief Financial Officer (CFO) and their roles and controls over the trading activities. They should have some say and in some cases final say on what an asset manager can do in terms of placing orders and using the **fund**'s money. In addition you should consider what aspects of operations may put an investor at risk.

It is crucial to follow the money and the way investors' cash is handled. A lot of frauds are linked to a lack of supervision or review of these key parameters. Essentially, investors should ensure that the manager's operations are serious and not dependent on an asset manager. Rather, they should be on the lookout for some validation of checks and balances. Very few investors seem to invest enough time to do this, probably as reading documents and checking that internal policies are abided by simply takes too much time and too many resources.

I have found that, on the other hand, there is an increasing trend for managers to have internal operational manuals. This is a good thing if such manuals are more than just for show. For them to be effective, the documents and processes they refer to have to be reviewed, used and updated including in relation to new regulations which are often forgotten. I have seen a number of cases where managers have created good internal processes and documentation, but failed to use them on a day-to-day basis. This is not uncommon as, after all, the application of processes is laborious and most people, especially in finance, ascribe too little value to them. Processes are too often seen as unnecessary burdens slowing down those making money. I think if you can detect too much of this attitude you can bet that at some point your money will be invested without enough regard for risk. That is a very strong warning sign. So how might you start checking front and back office operations whilst keeping your task simple and accessible?

Verifying the application of policies

One way for you to work out whether a manager actually uses his internal processes and documentation on a day-to-day basis is through an onsite visit. Although you might be able to obtain 70 per cent of the information on the fund's operations prior to meeting the manager and his team, you cannot, by reading alone, determine if things are being done in the way they are set out in the operations or **compliance** manual. I believe that an onsite visit is invaluable to your understanding of the fund's operational processes and procedures. This is your chance to verify that what is said is done.

Essentially, my kind of onsite visit goes beyond seeing and shaking the hand of the manager's key principals and a swift tour of the office. What is most important is that you talk to the back office staff and the accountants in the middle office. You must also be allowed to do so without the supervision of senior management. The reality is that the back office and middle office staff is where the real knowledge of the manager's operations resides. In addition, these staff members tend to be less trained to respond to investigative questions in comparison to the sales and relationship management teams. The middle office and back office operational staff also have better knowledge of non-investment related risks and will most likely give you a more candid answer.

When you review these operations and you ask key questions, it is vital that you establish the degree of independence that exists inside the control functions of the manager. For example you want to ascertain whether there is a clear separation of duties between those who take financial risks (the front office) and those who manage and control these risks (the middle and back office). As an investor, it is wise to consider whether investment committee and risk committee meetings are the norm and occur on a regular basis. The best way to check this is to see the actual recordings of these meetings, usually by way of minutes. This can be used as a source of information to see if there has been any decision taken in relation to investments or if there have been any amendments to investment guidelines or trading processes. If assets are hard to value you may look for a valuation committee as well, as this again provides an insight into how seriously questions of valuation are taken and whether there is a proper process behind them.

We can break this approach down by taking a look at both the front and back office workflows in further detail.

Front office workflow

Trade authority

From the front office you need to see who is allowed to trade and how any trading restrictions are recorded and supervised. In practice only a few asset managers/traders or 'executors' will have the right to pass orders. The front office systems should set this out quite clearly. You ought to be able to have a list of those who have the authority to handle the assets of the fund. You should also ensure that this has been communicated to the broker(s).

Once you know who has the right to spend your money, you need to understand how they work on a day-to-day basis, how they record what they do and how that information is passed onto their team in the middle and back office. Usually a lot of this is done electronically using proprietary or professional software.

Trade recording

The recording of trades as they are made is crucial as it allows those investing the fund's money to know what their trade book looks like, including how much available cash there is. Many a trading error has been the result of asset managers not knowing their exact cash position and overspending, so this is important. Proper recording will also give the risk management team access to the data it needs to determine if the trades are in line with the investment policy of the fund for example.

Common industry practices are still pretty rudimentary and asset managers/traders often type orders through so-called chat systems or through online brokerage systems specifically tailored to the corresponding broker or **prime broker**. Where a manager uses multiple brokers, the gathering of the information will be dependent on a number of different interfaces. The operational burden increases substantially, therefore, and this is made worse where trades are made over the telephone and not necessarily recorded in a timely fashion. This happens quite a bit too ...

The lack of good systems can be very perilous as a mistake that is not spotted sufficiently quickly can rapidly lead to a loss from which a strategy may not recover. Even a well-meaning group of asset managers/traders can suffer here. Regulators have picked up on this. I know that some of the systems used do not leave enough of a proper record and would not for example be sufficient to meet the standards set under the FSA record keeping rules.

The FSA record keeping rules require managers to record even instant messages. In practice, the rules are so detailed that it is unlikely that all relevant information will be entered into a chat system. In addition, the FSA requires a centralised record of all correspondence with the broker or prime broker. It is therefore necessary for the manager to have robust systems in place to ensure that trades are not entered in a way that leaves it up to the individual's diligence to complete all the required information. The records also need to be saved in a way that does not allow them to be amended. Some chat systems allow users to amend or even delete postings and are thus by definition not permitted under the FSA rules.

A good team of professionals with great pedigrees who launched a new fund some years ago suffered a major loss following the faulty execution of one trade that led to the fund owning a position that was much larger than it was supposed to be. This was an electronic trade and the error was human (also called a 'fat finger' error) – in effect an expensive typo. The error was spotted late and the trade had by then moved against the manager, which created a huge monthly dip in the performance of the fund. This left a sour taste for investors. Such an event makes it very hard for new investors to trust the manager's systems regarding any future errors. In this case, a more professional front office system might have highlighted the unusual position (perhaps based on its size) and would have prevented it if the trading system had included pre-trade position checks.

Robust front office systems are therefore essential. They also lighten the asset managers' day which means they can focus on the markets. Equally, they facilitate the back office's job. Good systems will allow for the monitoring of order flow and provide controls to avoid mistakes before they happen through a pre-allocation monitoring system.

Many managers regrettably are still relying on proprietary systems including manual Excel-based systems for much of the way they record their orders and positions. This increases the likelihood of human error, and it is easy to manipulate an Excel spreadsheet, thus enhancing the chances of abuse. This was done, for example, by a trader at BlueBay Asset Management, who was able to access the back office files and amend the information used for the valuation of his trade figures.

---

case study   ## BlueBay Asset Management

In brief:

- BlueBay Emerging Market Total Return fund was a £900 million hedge fund that took positions on emerging market bonds.

- Simon Treacher, asset manager of the fund, breached BlueBay Asset Management's internal valuation policies: he was accused of making unauthorised changes to information used to calculate the fund's **NAV**.

- It was discovered that Treacher deliberately altered seven documents and provided false month-end NAVs for a number of assets.

- He altered the documents by:

    - printing legitimate PDF version broker quotes that valued the assets;

    - cutting out and pasting different figures onto the valuation line(s);

    - photocopying the altered document;

    - submitting the altered document as the original quote.

- Treacher resigned from BlueBay in November 2008 and the fund was closed in the same month.

- Treacher's breach was reported to be limited and did not result in a material impact on the overall NAV figure.

- In February 2010, the FSA fined Treacher £140,000 and banned him from the financial services industry.

Lessons learned

- Errors of NAV calculations happen.

- Check for internal controls especially for hard-to-value assets.

- Remember that the **administrator** may not protect investors when it comes to valuation.

Knowing what systems your manager will be using should give you comfort but might lead you to question the choice of system or approach used. For example, later we look at the questionable and risky approach adopted by Amaranth's lead energy trader, Brian Hunter (see Chapter 7), which eventually took the manager down. I still cannot fathom how a good trading system did not pick up the risk put onto the books of that fund by Hunter, nor why that was not relayed successfully to risk management in order to limit relevant positions. In reality, most managers should use at least some of the specialised software that exists to control the flow of orders and resulting positions. There are quite a few off-the-shelf systems that include specific controls to prevent errors like a 'fat finger' error or unnoticed manipulations.

Remember finally that these systems are used at the level of the manager not the fund. The fund is not itself involved in front office trades but is only the pooling vehicle that benefits or loses from the trades. The fund's directors should ensure they know what the manager has in place, as they have delegated the responsibility for managing the fund's assets to the manager. In practice this is rarely reviewed at the fund level; the fund, as we noted, is too closely linked to the manager to really scrutinise any of these details.

Order management

In addition to being aware of your manager's systems, you may be reassured to see the manager's order routing chart. The manager should be able to show the trading process through a self-explanatory order routing chart similar to the one shown in Figure 6.1. This chart may look cumbersome, but it shows a clear process for any order that the manager is working on and how it should be followed.

Note that as part of the FSA rules, managers in the UK, for example, should hold information on their trading process on file. It is also good practice, if you are visiting a manager, to request that the investment staff demonstrate the use of the order routing process by opening the relevant files on their computers so you can gauge how it is really used. This should also demonstrate links to the back office.

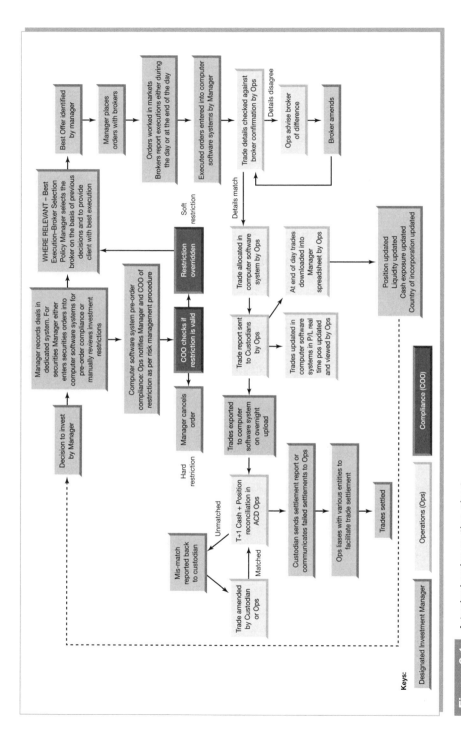

Figure 6.1   A typical order routing chart

The common way to record orders is through the use of what is known as a trade blotter. These can be recorded in various formats and were originally paper based. They are now commonly built into software solutions or are kept electronically in Excel spreadsheets. Surprisingly, a lot of managers still use paper trade blotters, which are physically passed on to the middle/back office for reconciliation. Even more managers still rely on Excel, which I think is not the ideal solution.

Back office workflow

Depending on the size of the manager, the back office tends to fall under the responsibility of the COO. The COO is essentially in charge of the manager's middle/back office functions, including operations, risk management, technology and IT support, as well as areas of accounting (although some of these responsibilities will depend on the work carried out by a potential CFO). The COO is usually also responsible for new systems implementation, some legal documents and looks after service providers.

You should always evaluate the level of the COO's experience and whether he or she is actually independent from the decisions of the main asset manager(s). Also enquire into the COO's authority or power of veto. This is always taken as a given but I know many COOs whose influence would be limited in the case of a disagreement. It is always useful to ask for specific examples of when a veto was used to illustrate that the COO has (a) made such decisions in the past; and (b) feels he or she actually has the right to veto.

So, what kind of operational activities does a typical back office perform on a daily basis? Below I describe some of the technical aspects of back office activities.

Trade reconciliation

Trade reconciliation is a comparison of information from two different sources, for instance the manager's financial calculations compared to the custodian's financial calculations, for the purpose of ensuring that both sources accurately contain the same data. This is usually performed by the back office on a daily and sometimes on a weekly basis. Different instruments can be reconciled at different time intervals, for example traded equities will be reconciled with the custodian of the fund on a T+1 basis (meaning one day after the trade is done). Other instruments can take longer. Sometimes it is also acceptable to reconcile cash levels at a less frequent interval depending on the amount of trading activity. What you want to see is a process that is followed religiously. Indeed it may or may not be appropriate to reconcile more or less frequently but what is clear is that if the manager says the team reconciles trades every two days, for example, I want to see that they keep to their own schedule. I can always opine later that the schedule lacks frequency but that may be a matter of interpretation. The actual reconciliation should not be a matter of interpretation but a matter of discipline. The day you miss a wrong trade it could take down the whole fund. As an investor I want to know if that day is likely to happen.

To get a better insight you might want to ask the back office staff some questions independently of the asset managers. For example, I find that if you ask the asset managers if they have had **trade breaks** (i.e. un-reconciled positions in their books) they tend never to have had any. If I ask the same question of the back office I usually get a yes. This is not necessarily an issue per se but it shows the importance of the segregation of those roles, and what can be gained from talking to the back office.

All of the above is true for all types of managers and every investor should have access to this type of information. For alternative funds in particular the roles of the counterparties, such as the administrator and the prime broker, should also be reviewed with regard to the reconciliation process. For example, you want to know whether they can access information from each other so that the process is efficient and the flow of data is seamless. You may want to check whether the prime broker sends trade confirmations directly to the administrator as opposed to relying on the manager who can otherwise meddle with data.

Valuation

The back office is responsible for ensuring the sound operation and control of the manager. This function includes carrying out a check on the fund's valuation process which is provided in some cases by the manager (see Chapter 5) and which is tailored to the investment strategy.

There is an inherent conflict of interest in the valuation process, since due to performance-based remuneration, the manager is incentivised to overstate valuations, and as a result raise performance and fees.

As part of the reconciliation process, managers are increasingly adopting fair valuation principles and establishing comprehensive documented policies and procedures. In addition, the majority of managers have moved away from internal valuation to independent administration supplied by third-party providers acting for the fund. This process of delegation can still be improved and it is still a work-in-progress especially for alternative strategies.

The valuation policy should detail the valuation sources available as well as any degree of tolerance for deviation in pricing and over-rides. This should be shared by way of an operational manual with the administrator appointed by the fund to officially produce the NAV and you could ask to see a copy to better understand the selected process, for example.

Cash management

The majority of cash held by funds is reconciled either on a daily or weekly basis by the manager's back office staff. When correctly set up, a cash management policy can partially help with the preservation of capital, improve the efficient use of capital which may otherwise lie dormant and effectively and promptly move cash around to where it is needed depending on the activities of the manager and the investment strategy.

Investors should consider how the manager handles the cash in the fund as of course there are risks associated with cash management. There are various options:

- cash can be left alone;
- cash can be invested in government securities, such as treasury bills or money market funds; or
- cash can be invested more aggressively in specialised cash strategies.

You should also check who can move cash from the fund to other accounts. This is a big part of operational risk and indeed where certain frauds started. For example, as I mentioned in Chapter 5, most alternative funds have some cash with prime brokers and traditional funds may have cash with various custodians even if by law the amount of cash is limited as the funds must invest it. Where cash is not invested in securities it is important to determine how it is held. Ideally any cash should be put into separate accounts from the rest of the fund's assets and segregated from other depository clients but this is not always the case and can be difficult to achieve.

History has shown us that poor cash management can have disastrous consequences. Examples include companies that invested in Sentinel Management Group, a cash management firm based in Illinois, USA.

---

case study   ## Cash management – Sentinel's fraud

In August 2007, Sentinel Management Group ('Sentinel') froze client withdrawals and sent clients a letter claiming it could not return their money without first selling their assets 'at deep discounts' and thus incurring losses. The letter blamed Sentinel's predicament on the 'liquidity crisis'.

The *New York Times* reported in August 2007[1] that the SEC filed a lawsuit against Sentinel one week after the letter was sent to clients, on the discovery that Sentinel 'fraudulently moved at least $460 million in securities from client accounts into its own and misused customers' holdings as collateral to obtain a $321 million line of credit "for its own benefit"'. Sentinel failed to tell investors of its activities of commingling, transferring and misappropriating their assets. In fact, Sentinel actually provided its clients with daily account statements that did not reflect the proper activities of the company.

One of Sentinel's clients, Capital Fund Management (CFM), was managing one of the largest French-based hedge funds in 2009. As a result of Sentinel's freeze on redemptions and uncovered fraud, CFM had to write to its 600 investors informing them that 10 per cent (equalling $407 million) of the French fund may have been jeopardised. CFM's **assets under management (AUM)** consequently fell by more than 20 per cent. However, thankfully on this occasion, within seven months they recovered the loss thanks to their performance.

---

[1] http://www.nytimes.com/2007/08/21/business/worldbusiness/21iht-senti-nel.1.7191724.html

Funds and more particularly managers adopt a common practice of listing who has the authority to transfer cash between the accounts. Investors should ask for such a list and at the same time keep in mind that cash transfers should have the authorised signatures of at least one (if not two) of the fund's directors in addition to at least two individuals from the custodian or prime broker. The requirement for at least two signatories is in line with best practice standards, so you should ensure that any cash transfer policies and evidence of a prior transfer all abide by this standard.

This should give you enough insight into the front to back office operations, a crucial part of the fund management world, performed by the manager. Once these operations are deemed reliable, of course the next aim is to ensure that the investment policies for the fund are applied with the same form of discipline and integrity.

The future balance of power between front and back office

Middle and back office functions are usually and quite unfairly lower in the pecking order of managers' lives. They are often perceived as a cost against the profit centre, driven by the asset manager and front office departments. This is a view with which we can sympathise, as it is arguably much harder to come by good asset managers than good back office staff. Having said that, good risk managers are pretty rare too and to demean risk management and back office controls is a huge mistake that continues to cost the financial industry greatly.

The back office responsibilities associated with risk management are crucial for any financial institution. If not technically a profit centre, I would still consider risk managers a cause of profitability. The job is one of control and that usually means dealing with lots of data. Their relevance to the fund's operations is highly significant, and risk managers and their staff can spot errors/frauds and save a lot of a fund's money. To look at things otherwise shows a misunderstanding of the investment industry and would be like going into a rally car race without a mechanic. Unfortunately there is still too often a culture of 'them and us' when it comes to the front and back office teams.

Salaries and rewards vary vastly and if personnel from the back office appear too demanding they can be viewed as a hindrance on profits and lose their jobs. It is my belief that this is still a prevailing view in the fund industry, exemplified by what was revealed during the financial crisis when a disregard for risk controls was found to have led to so many unnecessary losses. This was true for banks as well as funds.

Within small and mid-sized independent managers these divisions can be even more marked. The asset managers in the front office are often the business owners. They tend to have a disproportionate degree of influence over the middle and back office as employers, profit generators and owners of the business. The smart asset managers still put in place strong independent risk management processes led by operations managers who can confront them with hard facts. If that is not the case and this comes through during your review of a fund and manager, then you should seriously worry about the inherent operational risk that you might be buying into.

Funds of funds

Assessing back office responsibilities is not just relevant for funds with a market trading strategy but also for funds of funds. Funds of funds traditionally select the best funds for investors. This selection process should involve a lot of due diligence and a thorough review of financial performance and data but also of operational performance. One of the key concerns for managers of funds of funds is that a thorough review takes a lot of time and sometimes they just feel the pressure to invest as soon as they can. I know of a few funds of funds that, due to a stretch of resources and impatience, started making investments without carrying out proper due diligence. Senior management simply could not dedicate enough resources to onsite visits and did not want to recruit new personnel in operational positions. This is a huge cause for concern and it is still underestimated as a problem in the industry. It is difficult to imagine that the industry can grow without further investment in risk management and back office staff.

Back office relevance

We've all heard about back office responsibilities but they are often discredited as non-profit-making operations. The regulator is also often spoken of as cumbersome and too remote to understand the problems of financial institutions. Just look at the current debate about regulating banks. Most banks argue that regulation would hurt their business. But they forget that it was their business that hurt parts of the industry, because it was not properly supervised.

If you consider the case of Jerome Kerviel, of Société Générale, he was supposedly a frustrated back office employee who had broken through to the front office and somehow defrauded the bank on trades worth up to €5 billion. He was found guilty by the French courts in October 2010 of forgery, unauthorised computer use and breach of trust and was sentenced to three years in prison. Société Générale said it lost money because of Kerviel's risky trades. Kerviel has a pending appeal due to be heard in June 2012[2] and remains free until the appeal is heard.

Kerviel was the bad boy of banking but, in the end, he was just a person who must have known how to manipulate back office systems, which were probably too loosely set up. If he was indeed solely responsible for his deeds, then senior management is just as responsible, as he was far too free to act unsupervised. If a bank like Société Générale has difficulties in checking such rogue activities, then you can imagine how a manager, as a standalone business, is exposed to such a risk. Of course this particular case, which is similar to that of Nick Leeson of Barings Brothers, has been joined by the rogue trading scandal perpetuated by Kweku Adoboli at UBS. I believe that greater reliance on back office and risk management would have avoided these rogue deals on each occasion.

Summary

- The front office takes financial risks. It is important to understand:
  - who is allowed to trade;
  - how trades are carried out;
  - how trades are recorded;
  - how information is passed onto the middle and back office team.

---

[2] http://www.english.rfi.fr/economy/20111003-rogue-trader-kerviels-appeal-be-heard-next-june

■ The back office manages and controls financial risks. Typical back office activities include:

  – trade reconciliation;
  – valuation;
  – cash management.

7

Investment process and products

What topics are covered in this chapter?

- Investment process
- Key strategies
- A disciplined approach
- Dependence on research
- Using statistics and data
- Benchmarks
- Leverage
- Portfolio turnover and trading volume
- Market conditions and competitors
- Products traded and assets in your portfolio
- Capacity and AUM
- Investor analysis
- Principals' own investments

Although the fund management industry has many participants it is always unclear to me how much time investors have to check **funds** before they invest. In particular I was shocked by the alternative sector, which is supposedly limited to sophisticated investors, and yet many of them could not have been that sophisticated if you judge by what they bought pre-2008. In my view this is evidence that there is still a steep learning curve for investors to understand properly the key differences between various investment strategies.

I have heard many personalities in the fund industry claim that things have changed following 2008 and that professional **advisors** as well as funds of funds have improved the way they conduct their affairs. The evidence that anything has changed following the financial crisis is, however, weak. Even today some investors are still seeking to group hedge funds, for example, into an investment sector labelled 'alternative'. This in my view is naive and senseless since the variety of strategies managed by so-called hedge funds means that hedge funds as a whole cannot be considered to form an asset class. This was perfectly demonstrated at the time of the financial crisis when most equity hedge funds incurred heavy losses akin to those of mutual funds. Essentially, because they were focused on equities, such hedge funds were not really offering an 'alternative' strategy to the traditional long only funds. This goes back to the point I made earlier on correlation in Chapter 2: there were far too many investors effectively invested into the same sector, notably equity, via one form of strategy or another. There are strategies that are de-correlated, on the other hand, such as **CTAs** that did rather well for investors during 2008. The desire to categorise all funds under one label is, therefore, simply wrong. Let's try to be sophisticated in the way we assess the investments of any fund and understand how we can get the knowledge needed from a proper review of the investment process. This will help you challenge what you are told about the strategy of any fund sold to you and its benefits. It will also open up a few options when you are selecting, alone or with an advisor, the appropriate funds.

This chapter will give you a base to work from, and a few clues as to what you should be looking for as you continue your review of funds.

Investment process

When dealing with a **manager**, you should first understand the strategy offered. This sounds obvious but there are so many details that will cause one strategy to be different from another. To rely simply on the name of the strategy type used is just not enough. Let me give you some examples. In the equity world there are strategies that are long, long biased or market neutral. Within each of these categories you will have funds that are global, EU, Asia, Asia excluding Japan, etc. Within each of these sub-categories there are managers that employ individuals who wake up in the morning and choose their stocks by instinct and flair, others who will depend on information flow, and yet others on charts and statistics. Further, within each of those personal approaches, some will only cover large stocks, others medium or small stocks and then a few will change their approach half way through and trade all types of stocks. Your job, as investor, is to understand all the elements that make up an investment strategy. It is not easy, but not that hard either.

Key strategies

You can apply the above to all strategies. Although there are many strategies and styles of investing, the key strategies that sit within reach of most investors can be classified into four main groups with their sub-groups as follows:

1 Equity:

- equity long
- equity market neutral
- fundamental growth
- fundamental value
- quantitative directional
- sector: energy/basic materials
- sector: technology/healthcare
- short bias/long bias
- multi-strategy.

2 Event driven:

- activist
- credit arbitrage

■ distressed/restructuring

■ merger arbitrage

■ private issue/regulation

■ special situations

■ multi-strategy.

3 Macro:

■ active trading

■ commodity sector: agriculture/energy/metals/currency

■ discretionary/systematic.

4 Relative value:

■ classic bond

■ fixed income: asset backed/convertible arbitrage/corporates

■ volatility

■ yield alternatives: real estate

■ multi-strategy.

It is not always easy to understand or classify an investment style. The difficulty at the outset is trying to categorise any strategy. Very often even within a certain type of investment style, as I mentioned in the introduction to this chapter, no two strategies will be the same. For example, one equity long/short manager might be long biased (i.e. it will have more long positions) than another who will employ more short selling techniques. Likewise, two global macro managers may differ significantly in terms of instruments and markets traded, as one could trade physical commodities whilst the other could have more positions in emerging market equities. Most long/short strategies, for example, will not detail the profits made from shorting stocks (in practice this is rarely a source of gains). This is where analysis of the different types of strategies or markets traded will help you understand how the manager compares against its peers. The good news is that, despite these difficulties, some very basic checks will protect you. I still remember, for example, thinking that Weavering Capital (covered in

Chapter 4), which traded futures, was strange in purporting to follow a strategy entitled 'global fixed income markets'. That distortion made me very wary of that manager from the start.

There are many books about the trading styles of different managers and it is not the purpose of this one to reiterate some of the very good material that exists. What you should be concerned with here is the exercise of matching what is traded with what is represented to you. For instance, a manager may purport to trade European markets but you need to know what that means in practice. Starting with the basics and by way of example, what this means is that the portfolio is made up of European stocks which should be highly liquid. It may also contain stocks from developing markets depending on the definition of European in the legal documents, for example, where risks may be much higher due to lack of liquidity. Do not be surprised if you uncover emerging market stocks in the portfolio as this will be legal if included in the **prospectus**. I do not mind if the portfolio has developing market stocks as long as:

■ the manager is upfront about it and able to explain why (e.g. some opportunities from emerging markets are too good to miss);

■ I know that the manager is actively pursuing a risk management policy that deals with associated risks; and

■ the manager has appropriate expertise.

A disciplined approach

You should ask a manager whether it has any practice/set discipline in the way it makes an investment decision. Over time it is clear that the best traders, like the best athletes, are people of incredible skill who have the talent to train their minds to act in a certain way. The best way to train the mind, much like the body, is discipline so that certain actions become a reflex and emotions are taken out of the equation. If you can find evidence of this then you are doing well. Just as revealing is evidence of the opposite, and that is often a concern. This form of review is also a good way to appreciate whether the strategy will change over time (this is known as **style drift**), which can be problematic. The last thing you want is to end up with a manager whose style and approach are uncertain. Usually in difficult markets such managers are more likely to experience problems with their performance. What I prefer to see is an approach supported by a process backed by good operations and experience.

To dig further, I would strongly suggest that when reviewing the trading strategy you request to see the monthly newsletters dating back to the inception of the fund. I use those mainly to review the top five to 10 investments of the fund as well as a summary of its main traded strategies. Going back in time gives me an idea of what has changed since the fund started and how things might have evolved. This is particularly useful if I can see how the fund performed over difficult periods. I like to see, for example, how it reacted to the 9/11 attacks on New York or the attacks on London on 7 July 2005. These shocking human tragedies which affected markets in unpredictable ways can be very testing of asset managers. This form of approach gives you an opportunity to evaluate the consistency of the manager and its reaction to different economic cycles.

Once you are satisfied with the level of understanding you have about the type of trading strategy you are dealing with, you can take it to the next level by working out related concentration limits, sectorial exposure and how this is allocated in terms of the size of positions and why. I believe in facts and details when dealing with investment strategies. Use a technique that I have developed: whenever you read something about an investment process or are told about the more specific approach of an investment, you must always think of how what you are told can be verified or checked. For example, if the manager is investing in global equities I immediately wonder how the people involved can assess a very large world of stocks/companies. It will again depend on the approach and whether, for example, it is described as fundamental or bottom up. Both these approaches imply a certain type of work. Most investors do not make such an assessment and yet they have the means to do so as they have the knowledge and usually the experience. I find that investors get put off by the amount of time this process requires. There is also a lingering view that some asset managers are simply geniuses and this supersedes the need for any details. Nothing else can explain the extent of the Madoff fraud. There are of course some geniuses out there, but they are very rare and even they get caught if they do not ensure that there are solid processes around them.

So many investors have come to talk to me since 2008 about how they felt cheated by the investment industry as they lost so much money, not just in equity funds but also through large diversified funds or multi-strategy funds including hedge funds. I have noted that most of them did not check what the exposure of all their funds was in terms of correlation, nor the details of the underlying strategies that they had purchased to determine whether such strategies made sense and whether their performance was something that could be repeated in changing market conditions. Thus so many investors lost their hard earned savings in 2008 and will do so again if they are going to ignore the underlying details of the funds they buy. To some extent that was partially the fault of an industry that places a large degree of reliance on large banks or financial advisors whose incentives to advise may be entirely different from what investors expect.

The point remains that many intelligent investors seem to have avoided asking enough questions and did not take sufficient responsibility to protect their money. As revealed after 2008 most of the financial solutions that were sold were not understood by either the sellers who pushed the products, the banks which clearly did not control risk, and the regulatory authority that was shocked and surprised to find its industry in such turmoil. At the start of 2012 I worry that all the same old problems are still there. Not much has changed ultimately in the way people perceive risk and there is still a lot of reliance on third parties who themselves are not scrutinised for their work.

Checking the investment process is the only way to confirm that the manager is doing what it told you it would do and that it makes money according to a certain investment style or philosophy. Such an approach would have helped the investors who got involved in one of the largest hedge fund losses in history:

Amaranth

In brief:

■ Amaranth Advisors LLP was founded in 2000 in Connecticut, US.

■ It was mostly involved in energy trading.

■ The main energy trader was Brian Hunter. Hunter took large, risky positions on natural gas prices and made Amaranth a $1.26 billion profit in 2005.

■ In 2006, the opposite happened and Hunter caused huge losses.

■ In September 2006 bad natural gas investments led Amaranth to lose approximately $6 billion; it was forced to sell its assets at a loss to stay afloat.

■ Hunter was accused of seeking to manipulate the price of natural gas futures.

Founded in 2000 by Nicolas Maounis, Amaranth Advisors LLP was an investment advisor headquartered in Connecticut, US, that managed multi-strategy hedge funds. Amaranth managed approximately $9 billion in **AUM**, and was heavily involved in the natural gas market.

In 2004 and 2005, Amaranth concentrated most of its investments and capital on energy trading, led by a Canadian energy trader, Brian Hunter. Hunter placed 'spread trades' in the natural gas market and had high-risk positions on natural gas prices in 2005, the year that hurricane Katrina hit the US. Katrina had a huge impact on natural gas and oil production as well as refinery capacities. The trader made huge profits in 2005, and is said to have received an estimated $75 million bonus after his team produced a $1.26 billion profit.

Despite the fact that Hunter was presumably aware of the historical unpredictability of the spread in future prices for March and April contracts – which are largely dependent on the weather and socio-political events – he allegedly led Amaranth into further risky trades, probably in the hope of a repeat performance of his 2005 success. Amaranth apparently took the view that the price of March 2007 and March 2008 futures contracts would increase relative to the price of the April 2007 and April 2008 contracts. Unfortunately for Hunter, this trade was not a success. Amaranth's returns on natural gas plummeted; it had lost approximately $6 billion by September 2006 and was forced to sell its assets at a loss to stay afloat.

▶

On 29 September 2006, the founder of Amaranth sent a letter to investors giving notification of the suspension of the relevant fund's activities. Amaranth subsequently hired Fortress Investment Group to assist with the liquidation of its assets. Repercussions were felt across the US, particularly amongst municipal government and pension funds, which had invested heavily in Amaranth's fund. Furthermore, the failed fund led to increased pressure on the SEC to regulate hedge funds, as well as considerable debate across financial circles with regards to suitable risk management practices.

In July 2007 the **Commodity Futures Trading Commission (CFTC)** and Federal Energy Regulatory Commission (FERC) charged Amaranth and Brian Hunter with attempted market manipulation of the price of natural gas futures, including making false statements to the New York Mercantile Exchange (NYMEX).

On 22 January 2010, a FERC judge ruled that Hunter had violated the Commission's Anti-Manipulation Rule, as a result of fraudulent or deceptive behaviour. The FERC's findings were that for the three months between February and April 2006 Hunter purportedly created 'artificial NYMEX settlement prices by saturating the market with large amounts of futures and selling at lower than average prices during periods of diminished liquidity'. In turn, it was suggested that this enabled Hunter to benefit from swap positions on other exchanges. The FERC argued that Hunter's actions affected the price of jurisdictional transactions, and this was subsequently deemed as fraudulent behaviour. This case marks the first time that the FERC has found market manipulation by a futures trader. On 16 September 2010, Hunter challenged the FERC's findings at the US Court of Appeals but this was dismissed in December 2010.

Lessons learned

1 Be aware of the risks involved in a fund's investment strategy.

- When investing in the natural gas sector or any other sector, be sure that you understand the risks that pertain to it.

- Cross check the volatility of a sector using peer comparison to make sure you are comfortable with possible stress events.

▶

It is wise to consider the asset manager's style.

■ Hunter was known to enjoy taking excessive risks. Hence, investing in Hunter's fund involved exposure to additional risk.

■ Find out about the background of the main asset manager.

2 Be aware that high past returns mean high risk.

■ Hunter's 2005 success is as indicative of the risk of his positions as is his lack of success in 2006.

■ Check internal risk management policies and applications.

In my view, Amaranth's specific strategy was fine, as long as you could identify the consistency of the application of the strategy, both in terms of investing and in terms of risk management. In the case of Amaranth I cannot but suspect a weak risk management discipline and a hunger for returns that did not sufficiently calculate the risk reward on each of Hunter's positions. I believe that a careful study of his fund's broker statements might have helped identify the potential bets taken from time to time. I also believe that an interview with the team would have revealed a lot about the way Hunter traded without including all the prerequisite checks from risk management.

Dependence on research

Some strategies do not use research at all; others would be largely dependent on it. It is always good to get a perspective on where the manager you are working with stands on this and check the credentials behind the research. Research includes fundamental research, where managers are very much involved in information on specific stocks or market conditions. Some of this information, once public, will cause many managers to trade one way or another. You should always try to determine what type of strategy you are dealing with, and whether the research is an integral part of its success. If it is you need to trust that the potential for future research will allow the fund to remain unique. This means looking at the research team, and its overall contribution, in terms of process, to the manager's decision-making.

For strategies that are electronic or computer driven, research is almost invariably vital to the success of the manager and thus investors should check who does what on an individual basis. I found that in the case of one manager running a **commodity trading advisor (CTA)** (detailed below) the actual intellectual property used in the program managing the fund belonged to an entirely separate company based in another European country. On the face of it that might have been fine, but there was no contractual relationship between the two companies and thus no guarantee that these two firms would not part ways, thus leaving a potential risk for investors in the fund should the program no longer be available from one day to the next:

A CTA uses computer software it doesn't own

In this case, the manager had entered into a strategic partnership with a firm, which I shall call the 'Trading Systems Provider (TSP)', that developed an automatic computerised trading system.

- The TSP had developed quantitative software used by the manager, and produced quantitative research, reporting and web support for the fund.

- The manager covered portfolio operations, marketing, reporting, client relationships and some application development.

- The TSP and the manager were contractually committed together through a joint venture marketing agreement (the 'Agreement'), but had no detailed agreement between them with regards to the use of the software system that allowed the fund to trade.

- The Agreement in fact included provisions that clearly allocated the property of the software to the TSP, with few controls for the manager.

- More worryingly the Agreement stated that either of the companies could terminate the deal without notice or reasonable cause. So, for any reason, the software could be pulled leaving the fund with no trading system.

▶

As an investor you would have no control if this happened. You might not even be told.

■ From an investor's perspective, this would highlight:

- a risk related to the manager's dependence on the TSP; and

- concerns that the manager was not able itself to develop, maintain or improve the software system that runs the fund strategy.

■ These are the identifiable problems for an investor that could arise if the two companies stopped doing business together:

- A lot of investors might suddenly withdraw their investments all at the same time, thus causing stress on the fund which may have to liquidate positions quickly. This could ultimately lead to a potential depreciation of the **NAV**.

- At the same time this could lead to a suspension of redemptions and delays for investors to get money back as the fund seeks to slow down redemptions to liquidate the fund in an orderly manner.

■ The realisation of the above indeed may mean that unless the fund stops trading, it may incur losses as the manager tries to replicate the strategy through its own means.

In contrast, some managers dealing in more standard equity strategies, for example, use teams of analysts who pitch ideas to the main asset managers. Where this is the case, I recommend that you find out how much reliance is placed on analysts and whether that highlights any other risks. Obviously, it will also depend on whether the asset managers use external research, which is usually provided by banks. I suggest finding out the amount of time dedicated to research and cross checking that the manager has sufficient resources to keep that going. Key analysts are also important in this context and any departure would be deemed a significant change (see key man risk in Chapter 8).

Using statistics and data

One way to go about checking the application of the investment strategy beyond looking at operations is to use data and statistics on the prior performance of the fund. Some of the statistics usually provided by the manager or its representatives can be used for this. Assuming that the statistics provided are of sufficient quality, you should look at the relevant ratios and perhaps focus on the **Sharpe ratio** (which gives an indication of the risk adjusted returns) or if provided the **information ratio** (which gives an idea of how much return is produced for how much risk measured by way of volatility). These allow for the assessment of risk as against the fund's own returns or as against a form of benchmark. If the risk is high try to understand why. Many investors tend to be lured into a strategy by its returns and forget to consider the high incidence of risk which is revealed in these simple statistics. Be careful, however, to note that sometimes, some of the figures provided are themselves not correct. If you prefer you could subscribe to various databases that provide this information for investors and cross refer the various data sources.

Also note the reporting that is often supplied to investors on the fund's top holdings. Usually managers choose to report just the largest positions, which are not necessarily the highest contributors to performance. All the same, this can give you an initial confirmation of the investment approach and if you procure for yourself the historical information you should be able to check for any change in investment products or style over time.

Similarly you can use data provided on the size of the AUMs managed by the manager as this can often influence a fund's strategy. Some funds by growing in size make it harder for themselves to perform as it is more difficult to create the same returns on larger amounts of money.

Benchmarks

As you dig further into the process, another way to gain a better understanding of what the manager is proposing to do with your money is to test whether the strategy is aligned with what is represented. You can do this by testing its performance against various benchmarks and at the same time checking to what extent it is de-correlated. This is done by looking at returns and their distribution over time in comparison to actual market returns as expressed by a benchmark for the same period. Many investors I know do this using Excel by inputting all the monthly NAVs against any chosen index's monthly returns, which is relatively easy to do. Once you have plotted the data, if you note that the strategy on offer is too similar to an index that was not supposed to be relevant then you know that you may have to investigate further and ask more questions about the investment strategy.

Leverage

Leverage is the degree of borrowing a strategy will have. It increases its exposure to any risk of loss therefore. Leverage is not always easy to grasp as a concept and not all of it is from borrowing money. For example leverage is sometimes derived from using what is known as 'margin', which for all its complexities is another form of borrowing that occurs because the bank will not require the full amount of securities bought to be paid by the manager. The leverage used in any strategy is key to its success as well as its demise and must therefore be reviewed carefully. It must, like all of the above, be controlled with discipline by managers. The main issue for investors is that unfortunately leverage is a key factor in blow ups as it was for Long Term Capital Management (LTCM).

---

case study   ## Long Term Capital Management (LTCM)

In brief:

■ Long Term Capital Management (LTCM) was founded by John Meriwether in 1993.

■ It engaged in highly leveraged strategies.

■ In 1998 when the global financial crisis reached Russia, hedge fund market positions worldwide suffered.

■ LTCM collapsed and lost half of its capital base in a matter of months.

■ The US Federal Reserve organised a rescue fund, and 14 leading banks and financial institutions pooled resources and injected £3.6 billion into LTCM.

■ LTCM drew much media attention which led to the formation of negative perceptions of the hedge fund industry.

LTCM is a pivotal historical example of negligent risk taking that effectively shaped the way politicians and the public would view hedge funds. Following the collapse of LTCM in 1998, there was a public

▶

overreaction regarding the risks involved in investing in high-risk and potentially high-reward strategies in the wholesale markets.

LTCM was founded in 1993 by John Meriwether, a former senior manager of US investment bank Salomon Brothers. Meriwether recruited an impressive team of experienced traders and specialists in mathematical finance who built carefully researched mathematical models of the markets that it traded. By virtue of its model driven trading, LTCM's team avoided speculation on 'hunches', and therefore the risks that LTCM took were (supposedly) carefully controlled. LTCM also avoided insecure emerging markets and concentrated most of its trading with leading banks, preferring, for example, well-established government bonds. Despite the fact that LTCM borrowed incredibly large amounts of money, Meriwether felt he could calculate and control the risks taken.

LTCM raised a total of $1.1 billion. It supported transparency and provided investors with monthly NAVs, quarterly balance sheets and annual financial statements (which included full disclosure of off balance sheet contractual positions as well as frequent presentations to investors in relation to the fund's financial standing and prospectus policy). Today, such transparency and disclosure is regarded in a positive light as it protects investors. However, I believe that, in general, investors do not use the information provided to them.

Meriwether led the fund to an impressive initial success in the first two full years of the fund's operations: the fund accumulated an investment capital of $7.5 billion and produced a 43 per cent and 41 per cent return on equity. LTCM enjoyed enormous success until the summer of 1998, when unusually adverse market conditions dramatically affected the fund. In August 1998, the most significant factor that affected hedge fund markets worldwide, including LTCM's fund, was Russia's devaluation of the rouble and partial default on its rouble-denominated debt. The extreme unlikelihood of Russia's default meant that this event had not been anticipated. Although LTCM apparently only had minor direct exposure to events in Russia, the country's actions caused significant losses to Western banks. In turn, banks sought to liquidate investments that were seen as difficult to sell and high risk, replacing them with lower-risk alternatives that boasted better liquidity. The banks' actions resulted in LTCM losing approximately half of its capital base in a matter of months.

In September 1998, the US Federal Reserve System organised a rescue-fund for LTCM, and a consortium of 14 leading banks and private investment institutions injected $3.625 billion into LTCM. The injection saved LTCM from collapse and by mid-December 1998, the fund reported a profit of $400 million.

LTCM is a particularly unique and interesting case because despite incredibly high leverage and the excessive losses that were incurred, not a single LTCM employee was indicted for fraud, imprisoned or fined. No laws were deemed to be broken in LTCM's fund collapse, and negligence, malfeasance and bankruptcy were not deemed relevant. Today, the same is still probably true. The high levels of leverage post-2008 do raise red flags, but unless this becomes part of a shift in perception, negligent leverage will return. This case is therefore relevant in many ways and highlights the virtue of understanding the use of leverage, and its controls.

Lessons learned

1 Excessive leverage in any strategy must be carefully controlled for the worst stress events.

- Establish where the risk controls are, especially when you find out that there is a lot of leverage. Leverage will enhance performance to impressive levels, but when a trade goes against you, all that was gained will quickly be lost.

- Use statistics to determine the type of risk you face for the type of returns that you are getting. The risk levels are an indicator of what you can lose too.

2 Independent checks on managers/traders should be performed.

- Roger Lowenstein's book *When Genius Failed* notes that one of LTCM's weaknesses was that it had a weak corporate governance culture, all powers being in the hands of a few partners. He asserts that a major managerial weakness was the absence of any independent check on traders.

3 Better risk controls and credit analysis of hedge funds is required.

- The SEC and US Federal Reserve failed to consider properly the inherent systemic risks that can be caused from highly-leveraged non-regulated funds, such as LTCM, which was uniquely linked to so many financial institutions at the time, making it too big to fail.

LTCM, a non-bank counterparty, was allowed to write swaps and pledge collateral for no initial margin (a form of guarantee), as if it were a high credit-rating bank. The International Financial Risk Institute upholds that: 'Wall Street banks were collectively responsible for allowing LTCM to build up layer upon layer of swap and repo positions.'[1]

■ Look for strong independent risk controls.

4 Risk management practices must be in place.

■ LTCM had weekly risk management meetings. However, in his book *When Genius Failed*, Roger Lowenstein reports that the weekly risk meetings 'became increasingly scripted'. That is, the senior managers did not fully disclose information. You should always ask to see notes of risk meetings where you can to determine their actual legitimacy and value.

Since leverage is found in many types of strategies, I believe that investors have to better understand how it is used, whether there are any limits to it, and how it is managed by the manager's risk officers.

Leverage is even more relevant now, especially as it caused so much damage during the 2008 financial crisis and although the downturn is over, many of the market participants predict that leverage will cause new problems in any future financial crisis that we may face. If you agree that leverage and risk were miscalculated globally by nearly every single bank and/or fund, then it makes sense today to prefer to use funds that do not have any leverage or again ask for reassurances as to how it is managed.

Because leverage provides extra money for the manager to work with it will have a direct bearing on capacity and returns as well. It is therefore imperative to look at this in order to anticipate where the returns of the manager might come from in the future, and whether the manager will be tempted to increase capacity (to maintain leverage or simply to earn more management fees) whilst at the same time not considering that it will be harder to manage a larger sum of money.

---

[1] http://www.prmia.org/pdf/Case_Studies/LTCM.pdf

An understanding of all these considerations will reveal a lot about the potential investment and the character of those responsible for the safekeeping of your money.

Investors should, in this context, as they also assess the related so-called 'greed factor', question whether the manager is looking to continuously raise assets, despite this having an impact on performance. Managers tend to be tempted to do this to earn more of the reliable management fee. I like to know where a manager is with regards to managing its capacity thresholds and I prefer to see a manager growing the fund slowly.

Leverage

Now, it is a bit unfair to refer to a casino to explain leverage, but it is a pragmatic choice. Note that I do not think that managers gamble the fund's money; on the contrary they buy securities in which they believe. On the other hand the casino example is useful and simple.

Leverage is, crudely speaking, a bit like going to the casino with £100 and being allowed to gamble another £100 lent by it. So imagine that you win on your first go, you will have played £200 and say won 100 per cent; your winnings alone are £200. You now have £400 of which £100 belongs to the casino. Even after you pay it back you retain £300. Without that little lift/leverage you would only have won £100 on your original bet of £100. On the other hand, if on your first bet you lose the £200, then by default you will owe the casino £100 and you had better have it or the heavies will break your legs! In the financial world the banks expect the same thing, and will have recourse to any of your fund's assets if they have to find that money, as was the case with Peloton (see Chapter 8). They will pull the plug and make the fund go bust just to get access to some of the assets.

So for managers, leverage, which is provided by the banks that charge for it, can make all the difference. Your interest as an investor is that the leverage is controlled.

In order for an investor to better understand how to review the leverage in any fund I would note that most strategies are not legally restrained from using leverage, as you read in Chapter 3. The level of leverage should, naturally, be disclosed by the manager so there is nothing wrong about asking some questions on that since it is such an integral part of risk management. Even if all you do is pool some basic data together to check the level of leverage used over time and on a year-by-year basis for example, this could be very telling about the potential risk to your money.

The manager usually makes representations, orally or through marketing documents, which have hardly any legal force as almost always they are preceded by a disclaimer (see my comments on financial promotion in Chapter 9). Nevertheless, cross check any references to leverage wherever possible and look to verify any claims through interviews or by reviewing broker statements. For example, a typical prospectus will tend to use open language when it comes to leverage restrictions such as 'the fund intends to borrow no more than X per cent' with X being usually a large number. The prospectus does not thereby impose any hard or fast restrictions and the fund has, consequently, a lot of flexibility on how the assets may be exposed to leverage. The reason the lawyers would prefer to work things this way is to protect the manager from potentially breaching more narrowly written restrictions. To illustrate the point, if the fund's prospectus notes that the strategy will not borrow more than 10 per cent of the NAV but, in fact, the fund under the manager's control consistently borrows more than the 10 per cent, even if only by a small amount, then there are grounds to argue that the fund will be in breach of its general restrictions. Therefore, even if the manager is not intending to use leverage, lawyers will tend to recommend that it uses broader language to protect itself and the manager from potential claims. I don't disagree that this is sometimes necessary, but over the years the limitations on leverage have become ridiculously loose and inefficient. In the end this hurts investors and the industry. Some reasonable lee-way should be expected but managers would achieve more by limiting themselves and controlling their risk more directly and under the pressure of a proper contractual agreement with investors – that is by inserting the limits in the prospectus where they would carry legal weight.

Portfolio turnover and trading volume

To determine a manager's focus and reliability of decisions, it is very useful to look into the way an individual manager is using the money in its care and how often this moves about. For example a manager that is selling and buying many positions in and out could be doing itself a disfavour, as the positioning can lead to overtrading and not to any constructive collation of gains. I would encourage any investor to carry out a detailed review of the trade book if possible to assess the turnover of trades and their impact (did they generate money?). I realise that this is hard to do and may not even be possible depending on the level of disclosure available from the manager. If you do have access, this information can be very revealing of where a manager is showing added value. It is also particularly insightful if the data allow for a proper performance attribution per products traded. For the most part you will only judge a manager by the monthly returns and not by whether it makes more money trading certain products over others. This is essential if you want to find out more detail about the strengths and weaknesses in any management team.

Market conditions and competitors

Every asset manager likes to believe he or she is unique. More often than not this is not true. In any case you need to get a sense of that and the best way is to compare the performance of the fund in question with similar strategies. You should be able to find out about comparable managers and competitors. The manager of the relevant fund should also be able to name a few of the more directly comparable managers although often there is a natural reluctance to name any manager that may notably be better. To find similar managers, use the internet and search by investment strategy type.

Once you have identified a few (four or five say), try to plot the monthly returns for each similar strategy and see if the manager you are looking at is better than its peers. More importantly check to see how that manager coped with certain events of market stress where competitors may have done better or worse. All these are tremendously useful indicators of performance and uniqueness and give a real insight into the skills of the manager when it comes to the management of money. This is of course not a perfect science as there are so many variables to consider when comparing managers. Such an exercise may nonetheless lead you to ask good questions of the manager's team. For example it might help you to focus on whether the manager had a certain view of the markets (be it through research or otherwise) at a given point when the markets may have experienced heavy losses and this manager did not. This might give you perspective and you can assess whether this behaviour is likely to be reliable, based on talent, uniqueness and evidence of a process or a certain technique from the management team. This form of peer analysis never disappoints and may even lead you to find other managers that are actually better, not just based on returns but on the overall approach to both gaining returns and avoiding losses. This form of effort also avoids being limited to looking at what is presented to you, which is sometimes not the best of what is out there.

Products traded and assets in your portfolio

In addition to the analysis detailed above, investors should be aware of which instruments are associated with which strategy. Random checks on historical documents such as trade balances and **prime broker** statements can disclose whether the manager is sticking to its stated objectives and in particular if this is in keeping with what the manager originally intended to do. In my experience it is always useful to check what was stated about the investment strategy five years before in marketing documentation and see how that is reflected in actual trading. During my professional experience I have come across contradictory information from various sources on a number of occasions, for example when an equity long/short fund stated it was not trading options but its trial balance statements showed that it was actually using them.

For even more details on the portfolio of the fund, the underlying positions can be checked by directly requesting the information from the **administrator**. The administrator can provide historical statements of profits and losses; hence investors should be able to review the administrator's data, rather than data supplied directly by the manager. This is preferable as it has unfortunately happened that some asset managers have altered data and or falsified records. In reality investors would rarely be granted access to the underlying positions of the fund based on the fact that many managers would prefer not to show their positions to potential competitors. Investors could, however, request to see, if recent data are a problem, the historical trial balances and positions provided by the administrator as this should be too out-dated to be relevant to competitors. As an investor you can look at the concentration of positions in terms of sector and single stock exposures, and note all the markets traded. This can really help determine again whether reality matches expectations and to ask the right questions about operational and investment strategy controls.

Another way to dig for information about a strategy, which differs from looking at matters connected to the process of the investment strategy, is based on a review of the assets held by the fund. A simple sample of the daily trades made by a manager that can be picked up from the fund's investment statements can reveal a lot that is not necessarily said in the marketing brochures. Not all managers will offer this information and sometimes, as you will see below, this is justified to a degree. Many managers, as I noted above, refrain from giving away their positions in case competitors steal their ideas. Since an old picture of the portfolio is just fine for our exercise, there is no need to complicate matters. I must emphasise that while there are no legal obligations for managers to disclose this information, it is nonetheless crucial for investors to request it. For those managers that do accept disclosing their trading books you can use the information to see that each order reflects the relevant type of assets linked to the strategy and identify the products traded. This will also show how products may have changed over time for the manager.

As an aside, I would like to stress that any refusal to disclose this information is almost never acceptable to me (again bearing in mind that you can select a time frame for the disclosure so as not to include any current positions which understandably should remain secret). An example where this information was not forthcoming was in the case of Madoff (see Chapter 1). Madoff is reported to have simply refused to provide any trading statements, which should have been a massive red flag. Had those statements been available (and you can see this from statements made public after the fraud was uncovered) they would have shown that his strategy held a lot of US treasuries. US treasuries had nothing to do with the strategy he was purporting to be using. Seeing this information would have given any reasonable investor a chance to get away. In most cases the information does not lead to such dramatic results but can still provide a very useful insight.

In one particular case my team analysed a manager with a global macro strategy that was supposed to hold liquid investments. Our analysis of statements found that the relevant fund held real estate in the portfolio, which by any definition is not a liquid asset. That worried me and more questions were asked about the risk measurements in place and why this was deemed to constitute a liquid part of the portfolio. In the end the manager recognised that this should have been presented more openly. It was in fact an older opportunistic investment which should not have been traded. I liked the final answer but it did cause me to wonder about the future of the investment strategy if the past had held evidence of what I might call strategy distortion.

On another occasion, and as mentioned earlier in Chapter 5, UK-based Weavering Capital was supposed to offer a strategy based on fixed income as indicated by the name of the fund, the Weavering Macro Fixed Income Fund. The statements provided for the fund showed that the strategy was actually invested in futures. You will know that fixed income traditionally means bonds and that therefore it is hard to associate futures with this form of strategy. Of course if it is just a name; 'fixed income' can mean anything that generates regular income. So perhaps most investors had found nothing immediately wrong with the discrepancy between the name of the fund and the actual investments. Having said that, futures are known more for their volatility than their ability to help generate regular income. The simple verification of the statements did show something useful therefore, not to mention leading to questions on how the risk associated with futures was managed, as the risk profile is vastly different for the two products. In the end this manager ended up defrauding investors. Having any insights into the products traded therefore is vital to compare with what you are being sold and to check against any deviation from the main strategy.

Capacity and AUM

It is always very revealing to ask about the capacity and leverage of a strategy in relation to total **AUM**. Capacity is the amount of money a manager can handle before the strategy might not be able to produce the same returns. In practice, it is often noted that new managers in particular might be fine running less than $50 million, but will find it a lot harder once their AUM increases to $500 million. The impact is usually a reduction in performance. This is reflected, for example, in a recent study carried out by Melvyn Tao at the Singapore Management

University which shows that 'small hedge funds outperform large hedge funds by 3.65 per cent per year after adjusting for risk' *(Does Size Matter in the Hedge Fund Industry?, 2009)*. The potential for diminishing performance is a point to note and is normally caused by the fact that there are comparatively fewer opportunities for the money invested to produce the same types of returns as before. Some opportunities are simply not accessible for the amount of money the manager has to invest. It is also, as most managers will tell you, a lot harder psychologically to manage certain orders when the amounts involved are so much larger. Thus questions about capacity do matter. Leverage by definition increases the AUM and therefore takes up capacity.

Capacity

Let's look at another aspect of leverage and its impact on the fund's capacity and therefore returns. If a manager with a capacity of $100 million had only $50 million of client assets it could have (subject to a bank making this available) as much as $50 million in leverage. On a trade gaining 10 per cent on the total amount invested of $100 million, for example, that would imply that it would make a gain of $10 million so this would represent a 20 per cent return on the original client assets of $50 million (less leverage costs not accounted for in this basic example). For this manager since it has a capacity of $100 million the more assets raised directly the less it has to borrow. To continue the example, if it has $80 million then it would only borrow $20 million so the 10 per cent result would represent only 12.5 per cent of the original client assets of $80 million. Thus as the total client assets increase, the potential for leverage reduces and so do the potential returns (as well as losses). It is logical therefore that as a manager goes on growing its asset base and leverage becomes less necessary, the returns will also be reduced.

A serious manager will have a set capacity which is a good sign with regards to risk management and is evidence of sensible management. For managers that tend not to have any view on their capacity limit, even for very liquid equity strategies, such an approach must be thought of as potentially showing a lack of risk control or at least a lack of awareness, depending on the type of strategy concerned.

Normally information about the growth of assets should be readily available from the manager. All the charts on AUM growth that I have seen tend to show a sustained growth until around the end of 2008 when most managers lost assets. There has been a resurgence in investments after that which has been subdued since the end of 2011. There are a few things to note from the AUM story for any fund. You can use it to check that growth patterns are in line with peers for a start. If they are not, that may give rise to questions about what else is happening other than performance that leads a fund to gain fewer investors than other comparable funds. On the other hand, and this is more technical, you can use the AUM and performance patterns to determine whether the AUM growth has led to a lessening of returns over the same period of time. This would be indicative of a strategy that is possibly beyond its capacity and which may deliver fewer returns as the assets continue to grow.

There is other information that the AUM will give you if the same manager runs different strategies. This can shed some light on the importance of their various lines of business and which strategies may take priority over others. If a manager has more than one fund, the size of each respective strategy may affect the resources that are dedicated to the smallest fund. Often these will have a smaller management team bearing in mind that the managers are remunerated much less if the fund is small; so you can see that the firm's overall commercial interest will lie with the bigger funds. These little details may be worth noting and can all be derived from simple questions on the size of the assets involved.

Using AUM as a source of information

One of the first and most easily accessible facts about a fund is its AUM and this information is usually stated in a fact sheet or a presentation. Note that this information is not included in the prospectus.

Size and honesty

As we saw some managers feel that the information they provide in marketing materials, which is not legally binding, can be relatively loosely given. Sometimes, as a result, information on the level of AUM is exaggerated. This exaggeration is done in more or less subtle ways. Easy ways to enhance AUM include adding any borrowed amount or amounts available through 'gearing' – a form of **leverage**. Another is to simply refer to the AUM for one fund but in so doing aggregate all the assets managed by the manager not just those in the fund itself. Worse, but also done, is simply to make up a number, which makes the manager look bigger and more institutional.

The good news is that this is easy to check. You can refer to the latest audited statements of the fund to find out the real level of AUM. This is therefore an easy way to find out if you are being induced unfairly by a marketing representative to invest in a fund that may not be as big as you are told. If you find that out, then you should be cautious as to what else is loosely represented.

Size and safety

The most famous funds will have billions whereas start ups may only have a few million. A larger fund should provide greater financial stability, less risk, and a longer track record than funds with smaller AUM. High AUM affects the amount of risk spreading and hedging techniques that can be used which should be a good thing. On the other hand, when the assets are very large, the manager is at risk of having to invest so much money that it will be forced to consider many different forms of investments some of which may well be more risky than what would normally have been held as part of the main strategy. Thus the importance, again, of being able to determine what the holdings of a large fund are, where possible.

Most institutional investors will also not invest in small funds as they are not allowed under internal rules to hold more than a certain percentage of a fund (usually 10 per cent) and therefore since their minimum allocation is larger than most (e.g. £100 million) they would need a fund that was 10 times that size to be able to invest. This means that a large fund is however subject to bigger redemptions for each large investor and the domino effect in the case of a panic will be more intense than for a small fund where private investors and smaller institutions tend to be more patient. This thus limits the potential cascading effect of a run on the fund.

Size and performance

Larger funds may tend to underperform smaller funds which is why smaller funds are often an interesting investment for private professionals. This performance is sustained by market observers including the following:

■ Lazard Asset Management produced a research paper in 2002 which found that: 'despite the biases found in the data, investors may gain enhanced returns by investing in young hedge funds if proper due diligence is completed. *Hedge funds under three years of age tend to perform better than do older hedge funds without necessarily adding to the volatility of returns' (Alternative Asset Strategies: Early Performance in Hedge Fund Managers*, Lazard Asset Management, Chicago).

■ Infinity Capital, a Hong Kong based fund of hedge funds produced a report in 2008 which showed that: '"*Emerging Managers" continue to deliver excess returns of up to 500bp per annum over and above the returns of older more established funds' (New Managers Try Harder*, 2008).

■ Hedge Fund Research (HFR), a Chicago-based firm that specialises in indexation and analysis of hedge funds carried out a review which concludes that '*emerging managers*, defined as managers with less than a two year track record ... *exhibit compelling absolute return profiles and have typically outperformed the overall hedge fund market' (Emerging Manager Out-Performance*, 2005).[2]

In addition, the size of a fund does not tell the whole story. Indeed, just as important is how the fund's size might have changed over time and the impact this might have had on performance. The *Investments & Pensions in Europe* magazine advises that '*when it comes to investment, big is not always beautiful. The performance of an actively managed fund can dip if it becomes too big*', 2011[3]. For example, I know of

---

[2] http://www.mannaam.com/sites/default/files/HFR%20Emerging%20Manager%20Outperformance.pdf

[3] http://www.ipe.com/magazine/fees-the-big-issue_38565.php

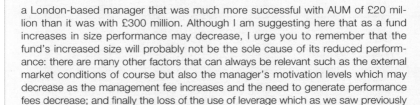

a London-based manager that was much more successful with AUM of £20 million than it was with £300 million. Although I am suggesting here that as a fund increases in size performance may decrease, I urge you to remember that the fund's increased size will probably not be the sole cause of its reduced performance: there are many other factors that can always be relevant such as the external market conditions of course but also the manager's motivation levels which may decrease as the management fee increases and the need to generate performance fees decrease; and finally the loss of the use of leverage which as we saw previously can have a material impact on performance.

Investors analysis

As you saw in Chapter 2, most funds are open-ended, and any investor can leave at any time. It is therefore up to the investor to know as far as possible who else is invested. Unfortunately this information is confidential. Nevertheless you should be able to obtain from the manager information on the types of investors and what group of investors they represent, for example, pension funds or funds of funds, private banks, family offices/high net worth individuals and possibly management/staff private investors. This form of investor analysis in relation to a fund can also provide plenty of information on potential risks or the probable sustainability of the manager as a business.

In the industry it is often thought that family offices/high net worth individuals are more reliable investors in times of hardship than the more remote funds of funds. This form of reliability could be helpful if the fund suffers a market event and loses money. Generally such investors tend to give managers more time to recover. This helps because if all investors redeem at the same time this causes another risk related to the need to sell the fund's assets quickly and thus usually at a lower price. This is therefore worth bearing in mind as you should prefer a fund where the investors will not all exit at once putting undue pressure on the manager to sell. You should also bear in mind that if one single investor represents more than a certain percentage of assets (usually in my view 25 per cent) this could create a substantial risk, notably in relation to funds being gated should you wish to redeem at the same time as the large investor.

Other aspects common to the fund industry are **side letters** or special arrangements legally binding the relevant fund to giving preferential treatment to some investors over others. Of course this is in itself a highly questionable practice from a corporate governance and ethical point of view, but it is not uncommon. There is some regulatory protection set out in 2006 by the UK's FSA which states that a failure by managers to disclose the existence of side letters is potentially a breach of the FSA principle that a firm must conduct its business with integrity. The FSA further states that *'as a minimum we would expect acceptable market practice to be for managers to ensure that all investors are informed when a side letter is granted and any conflicts that may arise are adequately managed'.*

In my view it was not until the 2008 crisis that the FSA started paying closer attention to the actions of UK managers with respect to side letters. In short, in the FSA's opinion, the onus is on the UK manager or advisor to ensure that side letters are disclosed. It is therefore always good to ask if some investors benefit from such arrangements which, for the most part, should only relate to (lower) fees, although sometimes they may relate to preferential liquidity terms. Other special deals may include receiving more frequent NAVs. Remember that any form of discrimination against shareholders/unitholders should be viewed as a red flag, as irrespective of its legality it is not in line with what would be deemed best practice.

Principals' own investments

As part of this investor analysis, you should check if the manager's members have themselves invested their savings in the relevant fund – Americans call this 'having skin in the game' as this is a very useful way to gauge whether the manager has aligned its interests with yours. It is important to trust your manager and in my view nothing invites that trust more than to know that manager's members have invested alongside you. Having said that, short of receiving a full list of investors through relevant administration statements, you will not be able to verify this information. I think it is useful to ask nonetheless and hope that the answer is true! Any manager not invested with you would be, in my view, more remote from the impact of the decisions that affect the fund. On the other hand bear in mind that for some **compliance** reasons, especially in larger banks, the investment team may not be allowed to invest in the fund. This is more related to the overzealous implementation of any compliance rule than anything logical or sensible, but it does happen.

Summary

- Consider the strategy offered and investment style and compare the main strategies that exist.
- Use statistics and data to check the fund's past performance.
- Test the funds performance against benchmarks.
- Look into the fund's leverage (degree of borrowing).
- Assess the turnover of the portfolio/trades and their impact.
- See how the fund matches up to its peers and market conditions.
- Regarding the products traded and assets in your portfolio:
    - check that the manager sticks to its stated objectives;
    - look at capacity and AUM;
    - find out if the manager's members have also invested in the fund.

8

Risk management

What topics are covered in this chapter?

- Risk management processes
- Key man risk
- Market risk
- Valuation risk
- Liquidity risk
- Counterparty risk

If you want to understand asset management strategies, you should have a strong grasp of the relevant risks. This might sound obvious, but there are so many risks to work on that sometimes this causes confusion or simply limits the time you can spend on each item of risk, which reduces your chances of spotting where things can go wrong.

What appears dangerous to me is that, because of the many risks that are relevant in the fund management industry, many investors choose either to rely on the fact that a **fund** is regulated or has well-regarded service providers, or keep to a strict list of risks that they want to review for every fund. The danger of using such a list is that the majority of investors do not give themselves the opportunity to focus properly on the most obvious and vital risks for the type of strategy they are considering investing into, which could be for example, counterparty risk or valuation risk, making the whole list redundant. It is not surprising that such ignorance or passiveness leads many investors to invest carelessly, either directly or through their **advisors**, and that for many this led to investments in the notorious Madoff Ponzi scheme (see Chapter 1).

Investors have also shown an ability to forget risks that are (quite honestly) mundane, but equally as important in avoiding a fund blow up or in protecting long-term investments. For example, see the cases of Amaranth (Chapter 7) and Weavering (Chapter 4). This is why I think a simple education in funds can help investors go a long way on their own without needing any sophisticated tools.

So, how can you realistically start to understand and deal with risks that affect so many different funds? I could give you a neat 'list of risks' to check off but you can get that from many different organisations. Instead I prefer to give you advice based on concrete examples that should help you adapt your own approach on a case by case basis. Let us start with this: when you deal with a fund, you should mostly be concerned about the **manager** and what its teams are doing.

Why focus on the manager? Not that long ago most investors would only look at funds when carrying out due diligence. The manager was pretty much ignored, taking it for granted that it was only relevant to the investment results but not to the operational risks that might affect the fund. The focus on the manager for me is the thing that has always mattered the most. This boils down to the fact that there is a part of risk that is common to all strategies. Thereafter you can focus on the other risks that are specific to the strategy you are considering investing into. With experience, such strategy-specific risk management will be easy for you to review. The core will however remain the same and that will be the concrete guide that should lead you to making better choices.

In this chapter therefore, I am going to walk you through risks related to the actual investment process as it is carried out by the manager. By the end, you should have a much stronger appreciation of how crucial various areas of risk management are.

Risk management processes

I often find that although experienced traders might have the knowledge and the right attitude to run their own portfolios, they usually lack the business and people skills to run the actual business of a manager. This means that a lack of business experience can create a culture that puts your money at risk. If you are able to pick this up from the information available from the review of the basic points that I outline in this book, you could certainly save yourself from making a bad investment decision. You could still choose to work with a manager, as nobody will have a perfect business, but do so forewarned and invest accordingly. So, let us start looking at what you need to know from the overall process of risk management.

What is every manager (and advisor, if applicable) going to tell you about their risk management processes? I can tell you that it's probably going to go something like this: 'We have robust risk management processes which enable the identification, monitoring and mitigation of potential risks.' They will also tell you that where the fund or the manager is regulated, rules and regulations apply which determine the actions taken by the manager and that this should give you, the investor, all the confidence you need to have in their processes and reduce the need for questions. Of course I do not agree. Indeed, what you probably will not be told is that many rules related to risk management are in practice rather limited in that they are broad and generic and their interpretation and implementation is left very much to the discretion of those responsible for them within the manager. There is no real recognised standard, unlike in other industries. Generally, regulators have few insights into how risk management is effected by managers and carry out even fewer independent checks. For example, in the UK there is very little actual review of risk management and even less enforcement action. Although the FSA does what it can with its limited resources and has increased its review of some aspects of the industry such as market abuse, risk management is not an area where it can afford to spend much time, especially as funds are seen as low risk in comparison to the broader industry that they regulate. Further, it would be very hard for the regulators to review risk management as there is not just one way of doing risk management. Indeed the regulatory system is itself based on what is called a 'risk-based approach' which means that in effect the risk is to be determined by the manager. This allows any manager to put in place whatever its teams deem appropriate. The regulation usually goes as far as requiring that the manager should be able to show that it has gone through the proper assessments of relevant risks and that its resulting processes are in place but this is very rarely reviewed. Therefore there is still much left to be desired in relation to the protection investors might get from a regulated company.

Look at a very famous and extremely well-established fund that was supposed to have been the perfect success story for two former Goldman Sachs partners and blew up because of poor risk management.

---

case study   Peloton Partners LLP

In brief:

- Ron Beller and Geoff Grant, two former Goldman Sachs bankers, started Peloton in 2005.

- Peloton ABS fund had AUM of approximately $2 billion as at February 2008.

- The fund invested entirely in mortgage-backed securities, considered relatively safe as it would buy only AAA-rated mortgage bonds.

- Beller's team placed trades on the falling value of sub-prime mortgages.

- This led to a huge success: the fund won the Eurohedge Credit Award in 2007 for the best performing fixed income fund.

- At the end of 2007/beginning 2008 banks tightened their lending terms and the market for highly-rated asset-backed securities froze.

- In February 2008 the Peloton fund collapsed.

In 2005, two former Goldman Sachs partners, Ron Beller and Geoff Grant started a hedge fund company called Peloton Partners LLP. The firm was successful from the beginning, given Beller and Grant's Goldman credentials and contacts. In 2006, the Peloton ABS fund invested entirely in mortgage-backed securities, that is, bonds created by pooling together home loans from across the globe. Peloton's investment strategy was considered a relatively safe one as it would only buy the highest quality AAA-rated mortgage bonds, which boasted little chance of the customer falling behind on payments.

At the same time, Beller and his team were taking huge positions against the US housing market that the poorest quality sub-prime mortgages would fall in value. Peloton took short positions in these sub-prime mortgage-backed securities, and since the prices of those securities plummeted in 2007, the short position reaped huge gains. Peloton's betting strategy had clocked up returns of 87 per cent over 2007 and the fund won the Eurohedge Credit Award in the same year for the best performing fixed income fund. The $2 billion of equity in the fund was repeatedly leveraged four or five times over, giving the fund a portfolio of assets worth approximately $9 billion. The high-quality mortgages in Peloton's portfolio were used as collateral to back the leveraged positions.

Only six months after receiving the Eurohedge Credit Award, the Peloton fund blew up. In early 2008 banks began to tighten their lending terms and Peloton faced difficulties after the market for highly-rated asset-backed securities froze. When the price of 'highly-rated' ABX indexes continued to drop, Peloton's 14 lenders, including Goldman, Lehman and UBS, asked the fund to raise more money to top up its cash cushion. Peloton could not meet margin calls from lenders and this led to a rapid domino effect in which the fund lost $17 billion in a matter of days and was subsequently wiped out. On 26 February 2008, lenders seized Peloton's assets, bringing a frenzied end to the fund.

After the collapse of Peloton, Beller criticised investment banks, stating 'because of their own well-publicised issues, credit providers have been severely tightening terms without regard to the creditworthiness or track record of individual firms, which has compounded our difficulties'.[1]

Lessons learned

1 Consider the fund's leverage position.

- The Peloton fund applied a highly-leveraged strategy, which exposed the fund to around 400–500 per cent leverage, and towards the end, up to 800 per cent leverage.

- Peloton borrowed heavily to boost returns.

[1] http://www.ft.com/cms/s/0/c5d43fb2-e62c-11dc-8398-0000779fd2ac.html#axzz1lyfwU8CX

2 Even the most successful funds are subject to collapse and market fluctuations.

■ Peloton like LTCM was so convinced of its risk controls and strategy that it had no consideration for the market changing rapidly.

■ The backing of major investment banks is not always a good thing; their terms for business are also usually the harshest and least friendly which means that when things turn sour they are not a good partner.

3 Be wary of the departure of key individuals.

■ In 2006 Peloton suffered the departure of three key individuals – Max Trautman (Founding Partner), Gary Link (COO) and Robert Lustberg (Trader), all of whom went on to set up Stoneworks Asset Management.

■ Rumours circulated that Peloton had grown too quickly (from $1 billion to $2 billion) and that it could not cope properly with its affairs.

4 It is safest to invest in funds that have a diverse investment portfolio.

■ Peloton's fund lacked diversification as it invested solely in the mortgage market.

■ The market in itself is known to be specific and complex, making the sector more concentrated and leaving little room for diversification in the case of a negative market event.

The approach towards risk management has changed a bit for the better for **UCITS** funds which now, under a new European directive (July 2011), must show more detailed risk management processes. This might even be applied by 2012 to long-short funds based in Europe. Nonetheless, even in this context, risk management is not prescriptive, so the end result will really depend on the quality of the team that puts together this risk management process. For you, this means that you have to check many risk related processes by yourself and verify that whatever is purported to be done is actually taking place.

You as the manager

I would like to use a hypothetical scenario making you the manager. Imagine that you are a manager, and regulations allow you to determine your own level of risks. Your risk-based approach is such that you do not believe that you are putting your clients' money at risk other than if the worst happened, which you determine as a very remote eventuality ... So you go about your day-to-day business limiting any interference from any risk related persons, other than for the basic checks on possibly meeting the investment guidelines (if you have some) and limiting any borrowing/leverage to the extent you deem reasonable or as may be set out in your contractual document if that is indeed the case.

Because, as a manager, you are relatively free to implement systems and controls that you deem to be appropriate to the activities and size of the fund, you believe that this constitutes a proper risk management process. You also know that senior management must ensure that risks are reviewed on a regular basis, ultimately making sure that the firm's processes are robust and continuously adapted to potentially changing circumstances, be they related to markets or operations. This is what the regulator and common sense would expect. Since senior management, as is very often the case, is part of the manager's leadership, you clearly feel involved in the portfolio management and as a result do not see the need for any more processes or internal checks.

If you appreciate this scenario, as an investor you can start to see the natural limitations that might exist in any manager. As a result, however, I hope you can also start to see what questions you should ask in order to appreciate what detailed risk management policies are actually in place. Since risk management processes should be written there should be plenty of easily accessible examples. Once you have the policies you can read them and verify that they are in use. Finally, following your checks on the risk management process implementation you should also ask for evidence of senior management reviews of the risks that exist for the fund. This should be part of the notes, reports or minutes of meetings.

In reality some managers may struggle to give you a written risk management policy. Many just feel that the risk controls lie with others in the company and that such people can use a computer system to monitor positions which they deem is fine as a risk management process and therefore not much more is written down about it. This is very often as far as the risk management process goes, and it ignores the many operational risks or stress test events that may put that approach under such pressure that it becomes redundant. If the manager cannot provide a policy, I usually find this to be a bad start. At the very least it shows that senior management has not deemed this to be necessary for the manager, which is poor management for a company that invests other people's money.

Sometimes, however, you get a good policy that covers many risks. Unfortunately even if you do get such a good policy, you will often find that there is no evidence of any application of it! It often feels very much like a manual on risk was put in place at the outset but is neither truly adopted in practice nor ever updated. On the off chance that you have seen all the risk management processes at work then you would also want to know if they are reviewed regularly by senior management. Their involvement is regrettably often rare especially if you have already noticed that processes and implementation are weak. Funds are there to make money, but also not to lose it. Caring about making money is one thing, but caring about all the causes of potential loss is another and just as crucial, as we dramatically learned again in 2008.

Putting it into practice

Now let's talk more about the ways you can go about putting the above into practice even at a basic level. To check that the risk management process is in place and is being implemented all you need to do is ask about it. For example, ask for any actions taken and recorded in relation to risk management, which you can cross check against the risk management policy itself. Usually a well organised manager will have some form of review and written notes that exist in relation to a risk that has occurred and how it was dealt with. If not then I think this is a weakness.

You could dig further into a manager's processes and culture with regards to risk management by checking how it deals with risk management overall. One good way to do this is to ask whether the manager keeps notes of regular meetings that involve all those in risk management. This is not about the reaction to a risk issue but more generally about risk management. Such meetings should occur in all financial institutions however informally. Meetings should cover any risks that have occurred as well as any potential risk and the managerial decisions taken to deal with them. I often get told that there is no such record of meetings. Usually I am not fussy, I say 'Look if it happens by the coffee machine that's fine too, but tell me there is a degree of formality to it afterwards, that ideas are noted for the next time so that there is some follow up.' Unfortunately I still don't even get that assurance. Managers tend to have meetings about investment ideas, not about risks.

Looking at this in more detail, there are two committees that are useful to know about in the investment management industry: the investment committee and the comparable risk committee. First, every manager has an investment committee which, in theory, reviews the direction of investments made by its traders. Yet, in reality, only the more established managers tend to have an official investment committee. Even fewer bother to record relevant proceedings in relation to the direction of markets or how the strategy should be applied if things evolve one way or another. However, even if you are able to get a record of the investment committee's proceedings, be aware that the majority of managers do not formally or regularly review investment policies. Instead, they make investment decisions on a day-to-day basis and as a result may feel that investment committees are not necessary. There is of course no need to exaggerate the usefulness of investment committees and some managers may feel that they slow things down and prejudice performance. There may be some truth in that but it does not justify having no meetings at all. Any reflection on a manager's actions can only be good for business and for investors and is certainly better than no reflection at all.

As part of good governance and risk management, in opposition to the investment committee there should be a comparable risk committee. A good risk committee would not just take into account the day-to-day investment decisions but would also incorporate controls in the operational framework that underlie the application of the management strategy. For example, I have seen risk reports that included a review of standard leverage and **value at risk (VaR)** limits, as well as deadlines for document renewals and procedures for the monitoring of **prime broker** margin calls. This gives you confidence that things are taken seriously and the broader the scope the better (within reason) as risk does lurk in many sectors.

Following 2008 you would think that the occurrence of risk management meetings would be a no-brainer but I can assure you that it is surprising how the overall culture has just not changed and how much risk, as a measure of success, is still being ignored. If a manager says that it has no records of the risk committee and it is based in the UK it can be very useful to remind the manager that this cannot be possible as a record of risk reviews must be kept if the company is FSA registered. Indeed managers have to produce certain internal risk reviews in relation to the **ICAAP** (the Internal Capital Adequacy Assessment Process). The ICAAP was taken from Basel II (the banking regulations) and is a very good process of risk assessment, which all managers must put in place. Unfortunately it is not reviewed or enforced by the regulator, unless the manager is of substantial size. It is very useful for investors to know about the ICAAP and it is a great source of information.

There are four crucial areas in an ICAAP:

1   the assessment of risk (the identification and measurement of the actual risks);

2   the application of mitigation techniques;

3   the review of stress-testing techniques; and

4   the role of senior management.

Without going into too many technical details you can see that it is surprising that with such regulations in Europe we nonetheless suffered in 2008 ... and yes, this legislation has been in place since 2007!

If you are informed that an ICAAP is not available or cannot be disclosed for reasons of confidentiality, remember that the findings of such a review must be made public. For some reason this is called a **Pillar III disclosure**. You can, therefore, always ask to review a copy of the disclosure and see if it gives you information about the manager's risks. Some of the language in the disclosure is a bit dry, but it will give you an insight into the organisation you are dealing with.

So, what is the most fundamental thing worth figuring out from all of this? After your review is complete, you want to be able to walk away with the knowledge that there is a culture of prudence and risk management. Most importantly, it is vital for you to ascertain that there is a clear segregation between risk management and investment decisions.

Below I set out more detailed risks that I think investors should be concerned about. You ought to be able to understand their application in the context of your fund selection. I will give you pointers on how to review them. Nothing is rocket science and all of the below can easily be appraised.

Key man risk

Key man risk is exactly what it says: the risk that a key person's absence will put the fund's strategy or the manager's operations at risk. In effect it demands that you work out if there is a truly relevant person in the manager's team and what happens if that key person suddenly becomes unable to act or leaves. Although investors may not always be able to gauge this risk, it is a common one and certainly merits your attention. It does not take a genius to realise that key man risk is a frequently occurring risk because many funds are overly dependent on one potential individual, usually the famous trader or asset allocator. To give you an obvious example, this problem reaches even Warren Buffett (one of the most successful and wealthiest investors worldwide) despite the fact that he has, over time, built a team of great asset managers around him to ensure continuity well after his retirement. Investors are still concerned Buffett's succession is by no means guaranteed to be trouble free.

I think that the main thing about key man risk is, quite simply, to be aware of it. You can then plan in certain circumstances to retrieve your money fast if and when necessary. Take into account that, in most cases, redemption terms (as you read about in Chapter 3) are often inflexible and could be subject to delays through gating provisions. Therefore, the higher the key man risk the more careful you should be about investing in a fund that has limited liquidity. For example, look at what happened to the Gartmore Group when two of its asset managers quit during 2010.

case study   # Gartmore Group

In brief:

■ Gartmore Group ('Gartmore') is an investment management company that held approximately £21 billion in AUM in 2010.

■ In 2010, Gartmore lost two of its top asset managers – Guillaume Rambourg and Roger Guy – and subsequently Gartmore's funds and company share price suffered huge losses.

■ Guillaume Rambourg was suspended from Gartmore in March 2010 following an accusation that he tried to influence his traders into using specific brokers to execute trades, which is contrary to internal rules at Gartmore.

■ Following Rambourg's suspension, investors withdrew £1.1 billion.

■ After an investigation lasting almost a year, the UK's FSA cleared Rambourg of any wrongdoing in March 2011.

■ 'Star' asset manager Roger Guy ran the firm's flagship European Large Cap fund and was responsible for more than 30 per cent of Gartmore's profits.

■ Guy quit in November 2010 after 17 years with Gartmore. He disclosed that he was retiring to spend more time with his family. It is also reported that he was unhappy with the handling of the internal investigation into former colleague Guillaume Rambourg, who resigned in July 2010.

■ In early 2011, Gartmore announced that Guy's resignation had accounted for £3.1 billion of the £4.8 billion withdrawn by investors in Gartmore's funds in the fourth quarter of 2010.

■ Gartmore's shares also plummeted 15 per cent shortly after the announcement of Guy's departure.

■ Gartmore's CEO, Jeff Meyer, stated that Rambourg and Guy's departure had 'exceeded all [his] nightmares'.[2]

---

[2] **http://www.ifaonline.co.uk/ifaonline/news/1894888/gartmore-ceo-nightmare-scenario-hargreaves-investors-sell-funds**

Here's another thing: key man risk does not only apply to the manager's senior trader. It also extends to other individuals who may be solely responsible for certain critical functions, for example in computerised trading systems it could be the head of software development, in some funds of funds it could be the CEO and in some cases it might be the CFO or COO. Thus, when considering key man risk it is useful to broaden your investigation to examine whether there are any individuals within the manager who are exclusively responsible for any of the manager's significant functions. The litmus test is to check whether their potential departure could endanger the management of your assets.

Key man risk is reduced where there is duplication of roles and or processes in the eventuality of a key person being unavailable. Ideally, most managers will have individuals who are able to cover for each other in the event of an employee's short- or long-term absence. There may also be processes or redundancy plans to organise at least the orderly liquidation of a portfolio in the absence of a key person.

Market risk

Market risks are broad by definition and can be deemed so hard to predict that they are not given the value they deserve by many investors. Don't be put off by any complications, after all if it is hard for you it is hard for everyone. There is in any case a lot to be understood from the analysis of a fund's market risks and even if you only touch the surface of the relevant risks by endeavouring to work them out you will ask the right questions of the manager and gauge how it has approached the issue. It is again in how a manager approaches risk that you will find strengths and weaknesses.

A fund's market risks should include an understanding and review of specific market sectors. This could be in relation to the various financial instruments traded by the manager and held by the fund or it could be in relation to certain relevant geographical areas where the fund has positions. Both of these aspects are affected by changes to markets. A chat with the manager should establish whether it is, for example, investing vast parts of the fund's portfolio in Japan. If this is the case, here are two examples of what you might want to gauge better as an investor:

1 Is there an impact from holding assets denominated in the local currency? The answer of course is yes. Then you want to know if the manager monitors this, whether it has hedged that risk and how. If all of that sounds robust and can be verified, you are in a good place. If there are evasive answers or non-verifiable facts then you have to consider if the manager would do well in the case of a Japanese natural disaster that may not only affect asset prices but currency rates. Of course if you are investing in yen then this matters a lot less but generally your investments will be held in sterling or dollars.

2 Is there a risk of a market squeeze or stress event that reduces liquidity and what impact would that have on the fund's own assets? For example, Japan is a large market and even after a stress event such as the tsunami in March 2011 there would be more liquidity in Japan than in a typical emerging market such as Egypt. Having said that, note that a market squeeze would be worse for the fund in question if the manager is using leverage. This would create greater losses in the case of a need to sell assets quickly at lower prices as a result of a lack of liquidity in the market.

Most managers will have in place various tests that help determine the impact of market risks. If appropriate procedures, such as the preparation of regular risk reports, are in place, the monitoring of risks should be easily accessible. Why not ask to see a copy of these tests and reports? Also ask for the manager to include any stress testing that has been carried out. Remember that it is not so much seeing the stress test that will help you: for the most part, these tests are made on assumptions that you cannot control or verify. However, the mere fact that there is a valid stress test may be a good indication of the manager's culture around market risk.

To give you an illustration let's look at Bailey Coates Asset Management. This case involves a fund for which the manager failed sufficiently to protect itself from market risk. The Bailey Coates Cromwell Fund subsequently closed down.

case study   Bailey Coates Asset Management

In brief:

- Jonathan Bailey and Stephen Coates, both specialists in European stocks, established London-based Bailey Coates Asset Management (UK) ('BCAM') in 2003.

- Bailey Coates Cromwell Fund, was a long-short equity hedge fund which, according to the *Guardian*, 'specialised in taking contrarian views on companies across the world'.[3]

- In 2003, the Cromwell Fund won Eurohedge's 'Best New Equity Fund of the Year' and attracted $1.3 billion at its peak.

- The fund lost 20 per cent of its value in the first six months of 2005:

  - Risk management problem – the Cromwell fund was large and exposed to losses particularly in the US.

  - Losses were compounded by high leverage.

  - Bailey and Coates blamed speculators (for rumours of redemption) and competing hedge funds for short-selling the Cromwell fund's investments.

  - Investors withdrew approximately $500 million in one month; this led to a forced asset sale over a two-month period.

- The fund closed in June 2005; the remaining $500 million of AUM was returned to investors.

- Two months after BCAM failed, Bailey set up Copenhagen Capital, whilst Coates set up his own firm named Coates Asset Management.

- The manager's risk management processes and procedures should have focused more on the lack of market diversification, large exposure to the US and the impact of leverage on the overall portfolio.

[3] http://www.guardian.co.uk/business/2005/may/25/economicdispatch

Valuation risk

Funds should have in place a documented valuation policy and it goes without saying that you should ask to see it. Ensure that it is a robust policy and that a process is followed when valuing assets. This will help you check that investments are not likely to be overvalued. In addition to outlining the valuation process, you should also be able to pick up from the policy who are the individuals responsible for ensuring that the policy is followed. On a practical note, if the manager only invests in simple quoted financial stocks then you do not need to be as concerned as when it is investing in hard-to-value assets. The harder the assets are to value the more this will all be relevant. Note, however, that even if the fund you are interested in has 70 or 80 per cent of its assets in liquid stocks and the rest of its investments in less liquid, harder-to-value assets, the valuation policy will be very relevant again.

It is common for managers to have a valuation policy, especially since 2008. That does not guarantee, however, that it is followed or applied. So, this means that when you see a policy you should (if possible) get confirmation of who is responsible for it and ask for examples of its application.

Additionally, when I've seen investors in the past do checks on valuation risk I am often surprised that they do not ask for confirmation of an appropriate segregation of duties between those with valuation responsibilities and those with investment management responsibilities. You need to do this and get confirmation of the separation of these responsibilities. This is linked to the comments I made above on investment committees and risk committees. The bottom line is that where the manager is involved in the valuation of assets, there is a conflict of interest, as it is likely to want the fund to be valued upwards. Therefore, the responsibility for valuation should actually lie with an independent third party, usually the **administrator**. The reason why the administrator can be responsible for valuation is that it should acquire prices from independent pricing providers. Again remember that in Chapter 5 I note that not all administrators use independent prices, which means that you cannot rely on them alone either.

In addition the valuation risk varies depending on which type of securities the fund deals with. For example, each of the following securities has different pricing sources and is therefore exposed to different levels of valuation risk:

- Market priced securities are the easiest type of securities to value since the prices are publicly available, for example on the stock exchange.

- Hard-to-value securities are valued by special pricing firms, for example administrators with a pricing team and are therefore not readily available for investors to see.

- With OTC securities prices are not available to the public/investors because it is counterparties that agree on price terms although the most common OTCs will have readily available price quotes.

Liquidity risk

Liquidity directly affects the true value of the fund. So, keep your eyes peeled for this type of risk. Different investment strategies will have different characteristics with regards to liquidity: consider a couple of examples.

My first example considers an investment strategy in equity. A strategy invested in European equity should have plenty of liquidity and be easy to value. The reason for this is that the securities will presumably be listed; and assuming that these are stocks from large companies there should be plenty of volume available. A word of caution, however: if the relevant companies are relatively small, and include small cap companies, the strategy may be less liquid than you think and potentially subject to liquidity risks.

On the other hand, consider my second example: a strategy invested in precious metals. This would not be as liquid. This is because the market is much smaller, especially if the strategy is traded through commodities or related commodities derivatives.

Understanding liquidity risk is important for two main reasons: first, to protect yourself from undesirable consequences; and second, to use this information to corroborate what the manager is purporting to be doing. This forms part of the review of the strategy as a whole, and can include checking what you are told with what is written in various presentations or contractual documents.

It is obvious that an illiquid strategy will require longer redemption terms. This is fine as long as you understand why. If there is an illiquid strategy it will reasonably take longer to sell assets at the right price and thus it takes longer for you to get your money back. On the other hand, I find that generally a liquid strategy should not keep you locked up into a fund unless you are willing to leave the money with your manager for a certain period of time (which some investors will do with more famous managers). Ultimately what is acceptable is what makes sense. I can see the benefit for managers of keeping your money locked up, just as much as I can see why an illiquid strategy does not want to force a sale because of generous redemption terms. There is usually a reasonable middle path in all of this.

It is vital that you remember that all funds assume some form of liquidity risk, and this includes UCITS funds. Liquidity risk means that under certain circumstances some funds are perfectly entitled to gate redemptions or suspend them. Therefore, you must fully appreciate the type of strategy you are getting into and the types of instruments traded, as this will have a direct bearing on when you can expect to get your money back, especially if there is another financial crisis.

Counterparty risk

Are risks associated with the fund's counterparties (that is, the fund's dealing partners) worth your attention? Yes, without doubt. This area of risk was virtually ignored until Lehman Brothers failed. Yet not so long ago another financial institution of repute, notably for commodity trades, Refco, also failed taking with it assets of its funds' clients.

Usually, counterparty risk is to do with the fund's banking partners. They actually hold the fund's cash and securities, and are represented by the custodian or prime broker. Therefore, if the custodian or prime broker were to fail, the fund would, in turn, potentially lose your money. This happens.

Have a look at the Refco case in which a broker filed for bankruptcy and the majority of clients subsequently lost their money:

Refco

In brief:

- Refco Inc was a large Forex and commodities brokerage house based in New York.

- In September 2005 an initial public offering (IPO) of shares for Refco was made. The CEO, Philip Bennett, was later suspected of altering Refco's books to make the IPO more successful.

- In October 2005 Refco filed for bankruptcy from creditors after the announcement of fraudulent practices involving Bennett.

- Bennett was accused of hiding $430 million in bad debts. He is purported to have hidden the debts in an unregulated company, called Refco Capital Markets, which he fully owned and controlled.

- Debts were facilitated by loans from Bawag P.S.K, the fourth largest bank in Austria.

- The total fraud has been estimated at $2.4 billion. Less than half this amount was recovered for creditors.

- Refco's customer funds were held in **co-mingled accounts**, which meant that money was placed in larger accounts that held money from a variety of sources.

- Therefore, creditors could not claim their assets ahead of other creditors when Refco filed for bankruptcy.

- Creditors had limited legal recourse as a consequence, and clients with funds lost investors' cash.

Lessons learned

- Be aware of your fund's counterparties and be ready to move if there are bad press reports on them.

- Check that the fund avoids co-mingled accounts.

So, in your research, in addition to being able to rely on the fund choosing a counterparty, you are now supposed to invest (your own) time and energy in checking out the counterparties! This is somewhat overwhelming, as in truth, could you really have determined if and when

Lehman would fail? Not many people did ... One way to protect yourself from counterparty risk is to review the credit rating of the fund's counterparties. It should be noted, however, that Lehman Brothers was still A-rated until a few weeks before its collapse. Therefore, although credit ratings may be good at providing a general indication of the long-term reliability of an institution, that alone does not suffice. I discuss credit ratings further in Chapter 11.

As Moody's CEO was quoted as saying in June 2010:

> If the future could be known with any certainty, we would need only two ratings for bonds: 'default' or 'won't default'. However, because the future cannot be known, credit analysis necessarily resides in the realm of opinion.[4]

Beyond looking into a counterparty's credit rating, I would suggest that you also assess the financial health of an institution by reviewing its financial statements. However, this might be rather onerous on most private investors and financial statements are often only made public a few months after the reporting period they cover.

So far, what I've told you about counterparty risk is that it involves onerous and time-consuming research. There is, however, the possibility that the manager does this work itself as part of its own risk management processes and you can check that. You could even see if it is willing to make its assessment available (perhaps by producing minutes of risk management meetings where such assessments are discussed).

Another alternative that became popular after 2008 was for funds effectively to diversify using more than one counterparty: a situation in which the fund ends up with more than one custodian or prime broker. In practice, talking to prime brokers where the issues are more prominent, I understand that this trend is slowing down as I write this book. The reality is that most funds do not have enough activities to make themselves financially interesting to most prime brokers, let alone two, when one prime broker is usually the focus of the trading, borrowing and other lucrative activities and the other is used just to hold cash, which does not pay very well.

---

[4] http://www.guardian.co.uk/business/2010/jun/02/warren-buffett-financial-crisis-inquiry-live

Another interesting development is that it was expected that investors would do a lot more due diligence on prime brokers. In fact this does not appear to be true. Recent anecdotal evidence indicates that very few prime brokers get asked any due diligence questions from investors. Even in instances where an investor does request due diligence on the prime broker, it is likely to be relatively limited.

Another final issue that would reduce the counterparty risk is contained in the legal agreements between the fund and the counterparties. Such agreements should be drafted in a way that protects the fund. Unfortunately this is rarely the case as most agreements provided by financial institutions are standard. Very rarely are they negotiated in practice by and in favour of the fund even if this has improved since 2008. You may want to review those agreements yourself, or confirm at least that they include provisions to properly effect the segregation of assets. Again the reality is that even if you did this and found out that the fund had not gone far enough in protecting its assets, very few investors would have any influence on changing any of the relevant terms. We discuss this in more detail in Chapter 5.

In conclusion, I am pushing you to find out if risk management policies are in place and are seen as being used and relied upon regularly. Some might say that a lack of evidence of a risk management process being in place is not evidence of the risk management not being in place. It comes close to it in my view. So be ready to be disappointed but this does not mean that you cannot still find a fund interesting, it just means that you have to remain particularly aware of risks that you need to account for. Remember also that it is quite normal for risk management to be weak: it is not a 'sexy' subject and is still viewed as a back office activity by money makers/traders. It remains a cost, often deemed unnecessary, for the activities of those making the money. I want to make it clear, however, that if risk management processes are lacking, this does not necessarily mean that you have uncovered a fund that is actually at risk. All I want to emphasise is that it does mean that the probability of a risk being missed or not properly dealt with is vastly increased. Thus in a situation of stress or a black swan event your money is more likely to be lost.

I believe that the reason why most funds lack or fail to put into effect robust risk management processes is because of costs. Risk management is expensive. You need people, systems and even more senior people to control that everything is being applied properly. Funds/managers prefer to limit those costs and thereby limit the allocation of resources to risk management. The reality of it is that there is still a lot of disregard for risk processes that actually should make your investment management strategy safer. Another reason is cultural: risk management can oppose the activities of the money makers by refusing to allow them to take positions that may be deemed too risky. When this is the case this affects egos and I know many a risk manager who has suffered more than a few frustrations. Again this is linked to the idea that risk management does not make money, investment ideas do. Whilst this is obviously true, only risk management can save a fund from losing all its gains. What you ideally would like your manager to tell you is that its risks and management teams are both part of the manager's success.

Summary

- Risk management principle – stay focused on the manager and its team.
- Risk management processes – it is wise to do many checks yourself.
- Types of risk to look out for include:
  - key man risk;
  - market risk;
  - valuation risk;
  - liquidity risk;
  - counterparty risk.

9

Compliance

What topics are covered in this chapter?

- Compliance status
- Compliance officer
- Systems and controls
- Financial promotion
- Financial reporting
- Insurance
- Business continuity plan
- Dealing and managing
- Anti-money laundering
- Prudential (capital requirement)

Many **managers** find that trying to comply with regulations is a burden on time and resources. Approaching **compliance** as a positive component of business management, however, can improve the manager's operations and avoid many of the problems, if not all, associated with operational weaknesses. Ultimately most of the regulation is designed as best practice guidelines. Some of it is not applied proportionately by some jurisdictions and thus smaller regulated firms, including managers, struggle to put in place regulations directed at banks or other larger institutions. The majority however is quite appropriate and can benefit any financial business and its customers. Regulations provide a structure that managers can conform to. In effect regulations provide a free guide on how to run a financial services business. Where regulation is principles based and not prescriptive, as in the UK, it is unfortunately not adhered to enough as we shall see below.

To understand **funds**, investors must look at the regulatory environment of both the fund and the manager, as well as the **advisor** where there is one. An **offshore** fund tends to have little regulation to comply with, especially in the traditional fund jurisdictions such as the Cayman Islands. In comparison, the manager (or the advisor) is normally in a jurisdiction with higher regulatory standards and therefore needs to implement and follow procedures and report to the regulator accordingly.

Compliance is important therefore on many levels including the fact that a breach of certain rules could lead to a ban from the regulator. This could leave your money without a manager, which would create an immediate operational risk even in the context of an orderly liquidation. So let me explain where I think you need to start with compliance, what insights it can give you with little investigative effort, and what to conclude about the various managers you might come across in relation to their approach to compliance.

Compliance status

There are as many regulators as there are countries, at least in the developed world. This does not make anything uniform and is not easy for investors to follow. However, since regulation is largely a matter of good business practice and common sense, the spirit of compliance flows from state to state. Note that despite the harmonised approach to regulation in the EU, European directives continue to be implemented by each country as it sees fit, occasionally leading to material differences.

Overall though you can work with the principles of good compliance and it is lucky that there are only a few countries that host the majority of funds and managers. Most commonly, regulated managers or advisors are found in the following countries:

- France (regulatory authority: Autorité des Marchés Financières (AMF));

- Luxembourg (regulatory authority: Commission de Surveillance du Secteur Financier (CSSF));

- Switzerland (several independent regulators, including the Swiss Financial Market Supervisory Authority (FINMA));

- UK (regulatory authority: Financial Services Authority (FSA));

- US (several independent regulators, including the Securities and Exchange Commission (SEC), Financial Industry Regulatory Authority (FINRA), **National Futures Association (NFA)** or the **Commodity Futures Trading Commission (CFTC)**).

Note also that there are no hedge funds in the UK, only regulated funds (although that may be in the process of changing), and that in the US until recently most managers did not have to be regulated. Therefore, when you are told of a hedge fund in the UK, that is simply a misnomer and such funds do not exist. It is the manager or the advisor that is regulated and that is in the UK. The fund's relationship to the manager as we saw before is one of delegation of responsibilities notably in relation to asset management. I say this at the risk of sounding obvious, because if you are going to find out about a regulated company you need to know which one you are looking for.

You should consider the jurisdiction of the manager therefore and whether the laws in that country require the manager to be authorised and regulated. This is the case for the UK, as we have noted, but not necessarily for Switzerland where regulation, other than anti-money laundering provisions, generally only applies to managers that are involved in managing Swiss domiciled funds.

In the US it is not always easy for foreigners to understand which manager should be registered with which authority: for example, if a manager offers and sells foreign futures contracts to customers located in the US, then the manager must either register or apply for an exemption to registration. However, for your purposes as an investor, you should note that if a fund is trading futures its manager should be registered with the NFA and CFTC (unless it qualifies for an exemption). So, it might be worth your time verifying any registration with both of these regulators. Note also that the US laws have changed and require that most managers register by March 2012 with the SEC.

The easiest place to start with regard to regulatory status is the information the manager has provided you with. The manager should have noted in many places, including its marketing presentations, where it is registered. In each case, you can quickly check the manager's status with the relevant regulatory authority. Usually, this can be done on the regulator's website at no cost. If you have been informed by the manager that it is regulated, but you cannot find evidence of this, you should certainly enquire further.

The majority of regulatory websites only list factual information such as the name of the manager and its registration number. Nevertheless, if you want more specific information you can request this from publicly available sources. Finally bear in mind that any check on an individual's name (see also Chapter 11 for more details on **background checks**) might also reveal their prior history including former employers and this is very useful in determining the past market activities of some of the manager's main employees. For example, in the case of Madoff, even well before the full extent of his fraudulent activities were uncovered, his firm was noted on FINRA as having been fined including in August 2008, February 2007 and July 2005 amongst others (see Chapter 1).

Table 9.1 includes some useful websites for you to use.

Compliance officer

As part of the compliance infrastructure, the manager must appoint a compliance officer who is responsible for the firm's compliance with regulations. In many jurisdictions the compliance officer may be liable if the firm fails to abide by regulations. You should therefore ask to meet the compliance officer so you can at least understand his or her degree of competence and independence. Very often, particularly in smaller managers, a multi-tasking individual may be appointed as the compliance officer. This general appointment tends to reflect a person with limited knowledge of regulations or at least with limited time to review and act in accordance with the compliance framework.

Table 9.1 Useful websites

Regulatory authority	Country	Website address
Australian Securities & Investments Commission (ASIC)	Australia	http://www.asic.gov.au/asic/asic.nsf
Finanzmarktaufsicht (FMA)	Austria	http://www.fma.gv.at/cms/site/DE/abfragen.html?id=KEWRWPF
Banking, Finance and Insurance Commission (BFIC)	Belgium	http://www.cbfa.be/search/dSearchFrmAdvFR.asp
Comissao de Valores Moniliaros (CVM)	Brazil	http://www.cvm.gov.br/ingl/indexing.asp
Ontario Securities Commission (OSC)	Canada	http://www.osc.gov.on.ca/Dealers/RegistrantList/reg_registrantlist-tc_index.jsp
Finanstilsynet (FSA)	Denmark	http://www.ftnet.dk/en/Tal-og-fakta/Virksomheder-under-tilsyn/VUT.aspx
Autorité des Marchés Financiers (AMF)	France	http://www.amf-france.org/bio/rech_SG.aspx?lang=en&Id_Tab=0 https://www.demarcheurs-financiers.fr/
Bundesanstalt fur Finanzdienstleistungsaufsicht (BaFin)	Germany	http://www.bafin.de/cln_108/nn_720486/sid_4346823671E0CB7 D5561CF95B0E0335D/nsc_true/EN/Service/Searchcompanies/ searchcompanies__node.html?__nnn=true
Financial Services Commission (FSC)	Guernsey	http://www.gfsc.gg/The-Commission/Pages/Regulated-Entities. aspx
Securities and Futures Commission	Hong Kong	http://www.sfc.hk/sfc/html/EN/intermediaries/trading/licensed/licensed.html
Central Bank of Ireland	Ireland	http://registers.financialregulator.ie/home.aspx?AspxAutoDetectC ookieSupport=1
Commissione Nazionale per le Societa e la Borsa (CONSOB)	Italy	http://www.consob.it/mainen/intermediares/investments_firms/index.html
Financial Services Agency (FSA)	Japan	http://www.fsa.go.jp/en/index.html
Financial Services Commission (FSC)	Korea	http://www.fsc.go.kr/eng/reindex.jsp
Malta Financial Services Authority (MFSA)	Malta	http://www.mfsa.com.mt/

▶

Regulatory authority	Country	Website address
Autoriteit Financiële Markten (AFM)	Netherlands	http://www.afm.nl/en/consumer/vertrouwen/bedrijf_bekend.aspx?sc_action=redirect
Securities and Exchange Commission (SEC)	Philippines	http://www.sec.gov.ph/
Comissao Do Mercado De Valores Mobiliarios (CMVM)	Portugal	http://web3.cmvm.pt/english/sdi2004/IFs/LPS/ei_lps_lista.cfm
Monetary Authority of Singapore (MAS)	Singapore	http://www.mas.gov.sg/news_room/enforcement/2008/index.html
Comision Nacional Del Mercado de Valores (CNMV)	Spain	http://www.cnmv.es/index_n_e.htm?english/consultas/BuscadorESI_e.htm~/english/p_inversores_5_e.html
Finansinspektionen	Sweden	http://www.fi.se/Templates/InstitutStartPage____6052.aspx?la=en
Swiss Financial Market Supervisory Authority (FINMA)	Switzerland	http://www.finma.ch/e/beaufsichtigte/Pages/bewilligungstraeger.aspx
Financial Supervisory Commission (FSC)	Taiwan	http://www.fscey.gov.tw/Layout/main_en/index.aspx?frame=16
Financial Services Authority (FSA)	UK	http://www.fsa.gov.uk/register/indivSearchForm.do
Financial Industry Regulatory Authority (FINRA)	US	http://apps.finra.org/rulesregulation/ofac/1/Default.aspx
National Futures Association (NFA)	US	http://www.nfa.futures.org/basicnet/ To request additional publicly available documents such as Form-8R submit an electronic form: http://www.nfa.futures.org/NFA-registration/PublicForm.asp
Securities and Exchange Commission (SEC)	US	http://www.sec.gov/search/search.htm Within the SEC website, it is recommended you go to the Investment Adviser search: http://www.adviserinfo.sec.gov/IAPD/Content/Search/iapd_OrgSearch.aspx
Commodity Futures Trading Commission (CFTC)	US	http://www.cftc.gov/industryoversight/industryfilings/index.htm

Therefore, it can be useful to understand how many staff members support the compliance officer as this will be indicative of the time and resources, and hence importance, the manager allocates to regulations, which in the end should support a better business.

I recommend that you do background checks (more on how in Chapter 10) and checks with the regulatory authorities on anyone involved in compliance at a senior level to determine their competence and regulatory expertise. Thereafter the usual tricks of verification come in very useful. Some are obvious, for example ask to see the compliance manual or the equivalent document that the manager should have. Then cross refer parts of it with what should be going on in the manager as this should be recorded. The manager should be happy to show you a lot of these records, evidencing compliance with regulations. Therefore, it is worth asking for them and assessing how readily the manager can produce the information. Information on these compliance checks is detailed further below in the section 'Systems and controls' which are the technical terms for what is effectively compliance application.

Systems and controls

Many regulators impose requirements on managers which stipulate the procedures they must have in relation to a number of areas. These include, but are not limited to, how the manager deals with its clients, on which matters the manager should report to the regulator, the risk management systems the manager should have in place, the training the manager should provide to its employees and other requirements such as the review of employees and the clarification of their roles and responsibilities. I love the two words 'systems' and 'controls' as they explain it all so simply. It is indeed about having a system or process in place and controlling or reviewing its application. This is what you and I expect any good business to do, including those within the financial services. Every business should put in place clear systems, lines of responsibility and deliverables, and should control them by spending time and energy on monitoring that the systems in place are being followed. So simple, yet with the way things are, some financial businesses focus only on investment ideas and treat the rest, mainly middle office, including compliance, as red tape and a burden on their activities. I strongly disagree with this approach and I believe even more deeply that if you are in the business of using somebody's savings the least you can do is set up a proper process and invest time and money in its review and application. This is essential to limit the chances of forseeable losses through weak operations.

Good governance, as well as many regulators, requires that a manager has a compliance manual which covers all these areas and details the practices of the manager. The purpose of a manual is not to summarise the relevant regulations, but to outline the procedures the manager and the individuals working for the manager should undertake in order to ensure compliance. When carrying out your review of a manager, it is prudent to confirm that the manager has in place such a compliance manual, and to see it, if possible, in order to check the accuracy of the information contained within the document and its practical application.

I often find that an outdated manual is already a reflection of a lax attitude to compliance, which most of the time is confirmed through later deeper checks. I remember a manager of one of the largest funds of hedge funds having an outdated compliance manual where even the name of the compliance officer, to whom employees are supposed to report concerns, was out of date by two or three generations of compliance officers! This is not good for business. Above all, such an approach will probably mean that weak risk controls are in place as the business does not appear to believe that corporate governance is as important as it should be. The reality is that, as I have emphasised before, a good business with solid processes will usually lead to longer-term sustained performance. When there is weak compliance the potential for errors is immediately enhanced.

Finally, like any system, a manager's compliance infrastructure should be tested on a regular basis. In the UK the FSA suggests that regular internal audits are carried out by external consultants or independent personnel. I strongly support such reviews and believe that proper records of those reviews should also be officially filed with the FSA and available to the public, which is not currently the case. It would immediately improve compliance as managers tend to take things more seriously when they have to file with the regulator. At present without such formalities investors are left in the dark or sometimes they bring in consultants to do such audits but this is very costly. It is a sign of our times that the regulation that exists is not used properly and we have to see the industry incur more costs to meet an understandable thirst for comfort from investors.

Financial promotion

Under normal circumstances you would expect managers not to misrepresent the performance of their funds. Yet in practice this is an area where there has been much historical abuse. Thankfully for certain retail funds this is more heavily controlled and generally financial promotions are subject to strict compliance. In the UK this is very much the case and recently the FSA emphasised the importance of the veracity of financial information and the limitations that should be put on disclaimers to avoid liability.

This topic is very relevant as it is financial promotion that is sometimes used to perpetuate falsehoods about funds and their management strategies. Expanding on what I discussed above in relation to the **prospectus** and linking this to marketing material, the marketing material that is widely read and studied does not actually provide much, if any, legal comfort. The omissions or exaggerations it can contain come in many forms and might even be, in some cases, simply innocent. Nonetheless investors should be well aware of what is sometimes seen in the financial industry. Let us take a look therefore at two examples of what to watch out for:

1 *Track record*: sometimes the track record does not relate to the manager itself but can be the principal's personal trading or trading with a previous employer. It is not always made clear that this is the case. Similar issues occur with simulated past performance. Sometimes this is made to appear as part of the track record, either with no indication that it is simulated or the disclosure has been reduced to small print or otherwise obscured. The fund should only have one historical track record that is linked to its activities from day one alone. Otherwise you cannot be sure how exactly the track record was obtained and it may not be comparable to what the fund is actually doing.

2 *Risk warnings*: notoriously absent, except for the classic 'past performance is not indicative of future performance', which is usually
buried in the disclaimer or stuck in a footnote in small print. Too
often it is almost impossible to gauge which risks are pertinent to
the strategy in question.

Financial reporting

This is one of my favourites ... easy access to insightful information at
all levels. Regulated managers must report to their regulators extensive
financial data and this will be the case in the US as well. Some data will
relate to AUMs and leverage, other data to standard financial reporting on balance sheet, profit and loss, and exposures to counterparties.
Regulators impose deadlines on the reports so you, as an investor,
should know that they exist. Nothing prevents you from asking for a
copy of some of the reports. This information, although not public,
should be readily available to investors. Any reluctance to share this
information might indicate a desire to hide certain facts that could
come to affect the manager's performance in the future.

Insurance

Within the world of managers, the issue of insurance needs clarification. Insurance is often misunderstood and in fact very few managers
have proper insurance cover, which for the most part is not manda-
tory for regulated managers.

Insurance is deemed important to cover and/or protect investors in case
of a claim which the manager may not be able to pay for. Note, however, that managers are not required on a regulatory level to take out
insurance. If they do take out insurance the cover level will vary and
there are no requirements as to what it should be. This is interesting
and by way of comparison in the UK, for example, a manager does not
have an obligation to have insurance whilst a law firm – however small
– must have £3 million cover. Go figure what is right! Nevertheless, this
is an important consideration, as I am often asked by investors what
is the proper level of cover that a manager should have? I do not have
an answer to this and I have come across insurance cover levels that

have varied greatly but according to our standards an appropriate level would be 1 per cent of AUM.

Normally insurance is taken in relation to professional indemnity, directors' and officers' liability, or key person's risk. Asking for evidence of the level of cover is very useful. Reviewing the fact of any cover will provide you with information on the limit of liabilities and what exactly the manager is insured against. You could also check whether the manager has ever claimed on any of its insurance policies as this may be indicative of past complaints.

Insurance, with its role as part of good corporate governance and compliance, should be reviewed and is an easy way again to gain some useful insights.

Business continuity plan

Business continuity plans are often required as part of the regulatory context. They are also good to have in place for any business. I like to know about them and the approach taken by managers when it comes to setting up and monitoring their business continuity plan. To understand and check such aspects of the manager may seem mundane but again reveals a lot about understanding the potential risk management and culture in place at the manager.

First off it is useful to find out if there is any plan at all. I don't mean some soft plan based on an undocumented idea of a back up being effected on a local laptop. I would expect a proper plan to be designed to save the manager's data at any time ahead of an unforeseeable catastrophe. I would also expect the plan to be kept in hard copy as opposed to being kept on the company's server, as what good is that in the case of IT failure! The existence of intelligent planning is always reassuring and shows good corporate governance. To properly guard against disaster and ensure business continuity, a manager should have in place a step-by-step plan that outlines the procedure to be followed in the event of a disaster. It should detail, among other things, the people responsible for actioning the plan, where the manager can relocate on a temporary basis as well as how to return to the place of business after the disaster.

What should be included in a business continuity plan?

Such a plan should include:

- ■ data back up systems of sufficient quality to deal with the level of data concerned;
- ■ recovery priorities for the firm's operations;
- ■ responsibility of relevant people in case of a disaster;
- ■ impact on market orders and existing positions;
- ■ communication arrangements for internal and external concerned parties (e.g. clients, press, relevant regulator);
- ■ protection and safe keeping of back ups;
- ■ offsite location or working area in case of catastrophe;
- ■ test to restore data;
- ■ test on timelag to effectively run the business again.

If you read most business continuity plans in the investment industry, it is still fair to say that they usually only tend to contain minimal information. They are focused on outlining the basic details of back-up systems and include generalities about certain principles and estimates of the timelag to re-establish the business. From what you read I think you can make up your own mind as to the manager's general approach. Note that the regulatory guidelines, notably in the UK for example, are not explicit on what type of plan should be in place. This is not an area that is included in regular FSA reports, only as part of the FSA application. You should also verify easy-to-access aspects of the business continuity plan. For example, if it refers to testing, ask to see a record of the last test results. This may give you a good view of the plan or indeed whether it is in fact tested at all. It is not easy for managers to do all these operational checks and many tend to forget. This is probably not going to be seen as a huge risk to the manager's business but when it could affect your money it is worth knowing at least how it is considered.

It is good for funds to know that the managers they delegate to have such continuity plans in place, as although they themselves are not expected to have a business continuity plan – as they delegate the investment management activities to the manager – they could be seriously affected in the event of a disaster that was not prepared for. Directors of a fund therefore have some fiduciary duties to ensure that the managers they retain have this in place.

Business continuity plans are also more relevant for some strategies than for others. For example a simple discretionary equity strategy that does not trade too regularly will not suffer as much as a high-tech trading system in terms of having to halt the business of the manager in the case of a disaster. The discretionary low-frequency trading manager can probably still contact brokers to change or exit positions and has time to do this. The strategy involving advanced technology trading effected by computers many times a day is much more at risk and had better have a quick and reliable way of getting back to business. So when it comes to it, you should focus on this aspect of compliance when dealing with commodity trading advisors and high-frequency traders. An adequate and efficient business continuity plan will ensure that in the event of a disaster, your investment in the fund will suffer the least possible disruption, as the manager will be able to continue business as usual very quickly.

Dealing and managing

There are three main compliance aspects that merit attention when it comes to understanding how a manager is dealing and managing your money. The first is concerned with the allocation of trades and the fact that your money should not be prejudiced by favouritism when a manager allocates its trades to its various client accounts.

Very often and legitimately a manager will trade accounts for various clients, including possibly some accounts for related parties or even itself. The starting point as far as investors are concerned should be that all accounts are traded equally in proportion to their size. This is the best way to avoid any conflict and this is called trading accounts *pari passu* which is Latin for 'on an equal footing'. Now, unfortunately in practice we know this may not be possible as some accounts may have slightly different strategies or some may be smaller and therefore not able to afford certain positions.

The key is for investors to appreciate that this represents a real issue if not treated well by the manager. Managers may justify that they have to use some discretion but the approach that they take should be reliable and consistent. Your concern as an investor is that, when things are tough in particular, a manager may have an interest in keeping one account doing better than others. There are many reasons for this, one of which is to maintain the track record of a flagship fund and another is that there is some special interest in keeping the fund that pays most performance fees gaining the most. In such a scenario, the manager may choose to allocate winning trades to the account that should do 'better'. This leaves you at risk if it is not your account/fund. That is why the manager should have a policy to reflect its approach to such issues and you should be able to review it. When you get the policy (which is usually in the compliance manual) you should check it for what is fair and reasonable and ask yourself whether in the case of the manager at hand, it may have a reason to treat one account better than another.

The regulator is aware of such issues. As such it is generally suggested by regulators and certain industry bodies that any market trade is allocated to an account before the result of the trade is known. This is called a 'pre-allocation of trade' policy. It is not actually compulsory in most jurisdictions, and sometimes the only requirement is that a policy is in place within the manager, but this is not checked. Regardless of what the law or the regulator might say, it strikes me as common sense and good corporate governance for senior management to prefer to have a dealing and management policy that addresses this issue; and one should expect to be able to get hold of it and review its application. To have such a policy in place would also help protect the manager in case of a law suit.

If you are still unsure how trade allocation affects you let me illustrate the point with the following example.

How trade allocation affects you

Imagine that you bought 10 lottery tickets for 10 children and you chose which of those children gets which prize as the tickets and prizes are announced. You might, even with the best intentions in the world, end up discriminating or showing favouritism if, as the prizes are announced, you decide to which child they should go, especially if one of those children is yours. The only way to avoid this would be to pre-allocate the tickets before the lottery results. This analogy, although simplistic, works well and demonstrates part of the issues. Normally within a manager, a trade is done or an order placed which gives rise to a **ticket** in front office speech. The trade has to be booked to an account and for various reasons this can sometimes be done after the trade is closed and the result of the trade is known.

I actually believe that this issue is so important that specific disclosures of the manager should be more clearly required by regulators in relation to the existence of such conflicts in trade allocations. For example, the FSA does require disclosures about the risk of aggregating orders but it does not require detailed prescriptive disclosures so this is dealt with by way of a generic disclosure clause, which is probably rarely read. In my section on the prospectus in Chapter 3 I comment on the fact that legally the fund and the manager seek to exclude any liability when acting in the case of a conflict of interest. This potentially covers the field of trade allocation. You can see that the fund and the manager appear to be protected should they inadvertently or deliberately abuse their potential position whilst investors are not protected. If more prescriptive disclosures forced managers to show where they may not follow a *pari passu* policy and why, I think this would help investors to at least be aware of the problems. The FSA in the UK does require a disclosure to the client when the firm cannot exclude a risk of material damage to the client. The FSA further requires that a disclosure of conflict of interests, even of the fact that a manager cannot exclude a risk of material damage to the client, does not exempt the manager from maintaining systems to prevent such a risk. In other words, a disclosure is not a free pass to risk taking and the FSA may take action against the manager. I do not know of many managers that are concerned with this risk even if the FSA clearly states that a regulated company cannot exclude a liability it owes to a client under the regulatory system. Before things change, and regardless of the relevant jurisdiction, investors ought to understand the issue and carefully review and cross check any policy on dealing and managing investments.

I hope I have clarified the issue of trade allocation and how it can be made worse if the manager's staff also have their own money invested in some account that they are trading.

The second compliance issue is better known and relates to trades that the manager's staff may do in their private accounts. Some individuals within the manager might indeed wish to trade certain securities for their own account. After all if you look at the markets all day you may have your own ideas which are not necessarily relevant to your day job. In practice this is nonetheless problematic as some staff may have access to information regarding the activities of the manager and its clients which gives them an unfair advantage over other market players/investors. For example, if a trader that worked for a manager knew that he or his colleague was going to place a large order for a stock, the price of which might be affected by the size of his order, he might place an order on his own account just before placing the large order for the fund. If it was a buy order for instance, he would expect the demand for the stock to increase its price and his account would have thereby benefited.

Managers have a choice of either prohibiting all internal trading, or trading that is concerned with securities that the manager is trading in, or in relation to securities for which the manager may have special access to information. The regulator has much more recourse against abuses of this type and managers in most jurisdictions must have clearly stated policies which must be reviewed and enforced. So why not ask to see them and verify their application? This would mean that the manager can guarantee that you will not be surprised by any abuse that leads to regulatory investigations and possible prosecution – none of which would be good for the performance of your money, as usually investigations are followed by large requests for redemptions and the closure of the fund which may be delayed by **gates** and so on. Such an example of insider trading which had disastrous consequences for the perpetrators was seen in October 2009 when Union Bancaire Privée (UBP) liquidated its **UCITS** III New Castle Market Neutral US Equity Fund – which had been launched just three months earlier – after the fund's asset manager, Mark Kurland, was charged with insider trading alongside Galleon Group founder Raj Rajaratnam. In the end, although the New Castle Market Neutral US Equity Fund was not directly affected, the news of the connection led to its closure. Rajaratnam's charges for insider trading together with several other Galleon employees are particularly noteworthy as their actions spurred the biggest Wall Street insider trading investigation in decades.

case study   Galleon Group

In brief:

■ Galleon Group ('Galleon') was founded by Raj Rajaratnam in January 1997 and specialised in investments in technology stocks.

■ Galleon was one of the largest hedge fund management firms worldwide, with approximately $7 billion in AUM before closing in October 2009.

■ In October 2009, the FBI arrested Rajaratnam in New York along with several other people for insider trading.

■ Rajaratnam is reported to have made as much as $63 million in illegal profits between 2003 and March 2009. For example, an FBI investigation found that between January 2006 and July 2007 Rajaratnam and others engaged in schemes to trade on the basis of insider information in relation to companies including Polycom, Hilton and Google.

▶

- Rajaratnam allegedly kept a web of highly-placed insiders in firms including McKinsey & Co consultancy, Goldman Sachs and Intel who leaked valuable corporate secrets to him.

- In a letter to investors dated 21 October 2009, Rajaratnam informed investors that he intended to wind down all the hedge funds of the Galleon Group. Investors received all their money back plus profits in January 2010.

- In May 2011 Rajaratnam was found guilty in a criminal case in the US District Court of 14 counts of conspiracy and fraud.

- He was sentenced to 11 years in prison and ordered to pay more than $53.8 million in forfeiture of illicit gains and a further $10 million in criminal fines.[1]

- In addition, the SEC began a civil lawsuit against Rajaratnam in 2009 and in November 2011 he was ordered to pay a further $92.8 million as a civil monetary penalty.[2]

The third compliance issue is one that relates to limiting the practice of making a fund pay too much for dealing commissions which it must pay to brokers who handle its market orders. This is usually at the instigation of the manager, which may have other reasons to let brokers benefit unfairly from the fund for which they trade. This was also even more common on personal accounts of regular investors. Regulators decided to act to restrict such practices (in Europe notably with the Markets in Financial Instruments Directive). You should note that, as a result, all managers in Europe should be trading using a 'best execution policy', part of which seeks to see a limitation on brokers' fees and notably to reduce the amount of friendly trades given by some managers to brokers that are close to them or returning the favour by providing some other form of service.

Technically the receipt of services or goods under FSA rules is distinct from best execution. Best execution has a discretionary element to it whereupon the manager can decide what is the highest priority (is it

---

[1] http://www.sec.gov/news/press/2011/2011-233.htm

[2] http://www.sec.gov/news/press/2011/2011-233.htm

speed, liquidity, price, etc.). Having said that, dealing commissions are strictly prohibited, as it is too much of an obvious conflict! Only if the services or goods provided by the broker are for the benefit of the ultimate client, can such a service or good be accepted. A best execution policy is therefore supposed to cover various aspects of what should be better for the ultimate investors. This policy can be requested and checked and will be more or less important depending on the type of investment strategy you are concerned with. For managers outside the EU you can still ask about their approach in relation to such matters as these issues exist all over the world. Ultimately a fund that is not protected by such a policy may incur unfair costs which will add to the **total expense ratio** of the fund and eat into your returns.

In conclusion to this section I would say it covers many areas and each of them can give you a very good insight on the risks to your money. Effectively when you enter into a relationship with a fund which itself has delegated activities of asset management to a manager, you trust that the manager will place the relevant trades to the account of the fund in which you are invested. You also trust that its employees are not going to abuse their position, and finally you trust that it selects brokers fairly and avoids paying undue commissions to related parties or market contacts unless there is a clear benefit for your money. A good manager will do all this. A bad one will not. In my view it is worth knowing who you are dealing with from the outset and all of the above can help you ascertain the character of the manager you will do business with.

Anti-money laundering

All authorised managers, at least in the UK where laws are quite strict, and to a similar extent in Europe, are required to carry out anti-money laundering checks on their clients. This is often misunderstood and for an investor the impact of a manager breaching its duties may not be too obvious. Such policies are supposed to cover clients of the regulated manager, and generally not clients of any fund for which they work, so long as an officially engaged party assumes this role. Many managers have, however, more than one fund as clients and sometimes, as we saw at the beginning of this book, the client is actually an intermediary management company itself based offshore. A potential investor should ascertain the extent and efficiency of a manager's anti-money laundering checks and procedures. If these measures are insufficient and the manager potentially facilitates money laundering by accepting clients who are involved in financial crime, this could have a very negative impact on the fund. The manager's assets and activities may be frozen for example and that could have an impact on assets in any fund.

With regard to the investors in the fund it is, subject to any contractual provisions, the **administrator** that is supposed to carry out anti-money laundering checks. The manager should check that these are carried out efficiently by the administrator. In reality very few such checks are done by managers as this is not checked by the regulator. It is also potentially quite onerous and hard to do. Regardless, neither the fund nor the manager should have any direct liability for what the administrator is doing. The administrator through contract has its own responsibilities to the fund in this regard. For investors all it means is that you should check the manager's understanding of its obligations and ultimately remember that the potential risk of one investor laundering money through the fund could potentially affect all other investors.

Prudential (capital requirement)

You will have heard of capital requirements in the context of banks following the 2008 financial crisis. The same principles apply to managers where they are regulated. They have to have a minimal capital according to EU rules and regulations for example. The requirements have always felt a bit awkward and almost inappropriate in the context of what a manager or advisor does. Indeed the regular capital was set at €50,000, and I have never really understood the exact reason why this level was chosen by the EU. It certainly would not compensate for any significant losses in relation to fund management. On the other hand it does force entrepreneurs in the financial world to at least put up some capital before they start their businesses and this is a good thing as it probably avoids weaker businesses from launching. It also compels them to reinvest if they cannot maintain the minimum capital requirements, which could serve as a warning light to the regulator, and thus provide sufficient notice should there be any fundamental issues that cannot be resolved.

In any case the requirements regarding the minimum capitalisation of managers have changed substantially over the past few years and this mostly comes from the review of what are considered prudential capital management issues. One item that has emerged from this in the EU is the **ICAAP**, which I touched upon in Chapter 8. The ICAAP is an internal document that reviews the internal capital adequacy of the manager ... the last two letters of the acronym standing for assessment process. It is a useful document which you can ask to see. It should highlight any weaknesses in the manager and/or the way at least that the manager is attempting to address them. I sometimes use it the other way around and if I see that the manager assesses that it has no risks I view that as a weakness. It is an internal document and is not reviewed by the regulator, unless you are a firm trading proprietary assets. As such, managers and advisors who have to do this tend to do it as they see fit and although there are guidelines they are not terribly prescriptive, and are not always followed.

As such the ICAAP of any manager is not entirely reliable. In fact the FSA produced a report highlighting its concerns in January 2010.[3] The observations highlighted weaknesses for some of the ICAAPs that the FSA reviewed. The FSA's key observations are very revealing, especially considering that this is about firms that have to submit their ICAAPs to the FSA (which is not the case for most managers). So despite their potential failings, ICAAPs have their uses, especially for investors wanting access to easy and free information.

Summary

- Compliance is viewed by some as a burden on time and resources and by others as a positive component of business management.

- You need to consider the compliance status in the relevant jurisdiction.

---

[3] 'ICAAP Submissions – Observations for Limited Licence Investment Firms', FSA, January 2010.

- Assess the compliance officer, i.e. the person liable for ensuring the fund complies with regulations.

- Compliance systems and controls should be in place.

- Be aware of exaggerations or misrepresentations in financial promotions.

- Insurance – how far are you protected? You need to assess this aspect.

- Check whether a business continuity plan exists and whether it has been executed.

- How does the manager deal with and manage your money?

- Anti-money laundering checks and procedures should be in place.

10

Background checks

What topics are covered in this chapter?

- Relevance of background checks
- Practical steps

In this chapter I am going to show you how you can go about doing a **background check** on any person or organisation of interest, using your resources. By the end of this chapter you will have all the tips and insights that are relevant to carrying out this task.

Relevance of background checks

I mentioned the importance of performing background checks on senior staff of the **fund** and the **manager** earlier in this book, and as noted above this can be done on almost any relevant financial firm. It is amazing how much information can be found about asset managers and **compliance** personnel.

By way of example let's look at the case of Daedalus Capital Partners LLC, a hedge fund in the US, where some investors presumably failed to do the basic background checks on the purported asset manager and suffered the consequences of a fraud carried out by a mother and her son.

Daedalus Capital Partners

In brief:

■ Mother, Ayferafet Yalincak, assisted 22-year-old college son, Hakan Yalincak, to recruit US investors in a multimillion dollar hedge fund fraud and Ponzi scheme.

■ Hakan was a student at New York University. He had committed credit card fraud and opened bogus trading accounts in his youth, prior to starting university.

■ In 2003 Hakan formed hedge fund Daedalus Capital Partners with an associate, Matthew J. Thomas.

■ The scam involved the following:

– Fraudulent credit card transactions were used to raise capital for the hedge fund.

– To attract additional investments, the mother attended meetings with investors and her son presented her as a member of a wealthy Turkish family who was going to invest millions in his hedge fund.

– Hakan charmed Greenwich businessmen with phoney investment strategies.

– The fund did not exist and Hakan used fraudulent financial documents.

■ Investor money was used as a $1.25 million donation[1] to NYU and to buy expensive personal goods (e.g. a Porsche and jewellery).

■ On 26 April 2005, a Connecticut grand jury issued a bank fraud indictment against Hakan.

■ The mother pleaded guilty to conspiracy to commit wire fraud; Hakan pleaded guilty to bank fraud and wire fraud.

■ Hakan was sentenced to 42 months in prison and ordered to pay $4.18 million in restitution.

Lessons learned

■ Investors should have performed just a basic background check on Hakan.

■ Anyone who was involved in fraud (credit card fraud) would have raised suspicions.

[1] http://nymag.com/nymetro/news/people/features/12070/

Basic guidelines

Now let me tell you how you can do a background check simply by using your personal computer. Before you start your background search, keep in mind the following guidelines.

Starting off

Your starting point depends largely on where the **manager/advisor** is based. What matters here is the country or jurisdiction that will have the most information about the person you are researching. For example, if a manager is based in France, I would start by checking the French regulatory websites (the Autorité des Marchés Financiers (AMF) and Banque de France), followed by the French companies' register. If based in the UK, I would review the Financial Services Authority (FSA) register and details available from Companies House. Generally, and in any case, I always recommend that all the main official websites listed below are searched, so that nothing is missed.

Looking at the individual's employment history:

In addition to searching regulatory websites in the manager's current jurisdiction for the relevant individuals, you should look at each of their employment histories to see where else they have worked. If it turns out that they have previously been based in other jurisdictions, be sure to check the regulatory websites of those jurisdictions as well.

Obtaining general public information

Finding information always takes a lot of time, but in most cases it is available. It is, however, easier to find information in some jurisdictions than in others. For instance, in the US, the amount of information publicly available is vast and readily accessible, whereas in other countries, such as Japan, it is more difficult to find information, as public access is limited. It is also the case that some regulatory websites do not have comprehensive databases.

Cost and depth of background checks

As an investor, you have to consider how many resources you are able to dedicate to background checks. There are a range of costs, varying from a free Google search, which is just an investment of time, to databases that charge a fee to gain access to their information. Be aware that some databases may be quite costly. Also, if you were to decide to outsource your background checks to a professional company, this might become expensive depending on the depth of information required, even if it saves time and is done to a professional standard.

Deciding whether you want to hire a professional company

It might be worth outsourcing background checks to a service provider such as a professional investigations company. If you do, I recommend that you first specify exactly what the checks should cover, so that you can estimate how long it will take and how much it will cost. For example, some investigators verify candidates' CVs by confirming the exact dates of each job, as well as talking to each past employer. This is definitely more than you need to gauge the background of someone for the costs incurred. The advantage of using a professional company is that its staff are trained on the background investigation process and are therefore more efficient at reviewing and sourcing relevant information. It may also be that as an individual investor, you might not be able to access certain databases, including certain court databases, which are limited to professionals. Professional firms should be able to deal with all these hurdles. If you do appoint a professional firm, another way to reduce costs may be to buy an existing, albeit outdated, report. I find older data go far enough in most cases, and they are usually cheaper and readily available. If in doubt or if there are other checks that do not provide you with the detailed information you are looking for, use updated data, which will come at a higher cost and may take time to collect.

Access to private information

I like to cross check certain aspects of CVs just to tell if people are being honest. Individuals tend to exaggerate their previous experience and, if that is the case, then I highlight this as an immediate concern as it reflects poorly on the individual's character. The manager may, however, refuse to disclose the past experience of certain members of its team, deeming that it is too demanding or too detailed a request. I know of a recent case where an investor's request was denied when he sought a copy of a university degree from a manager based in Switzerland.

The investor was informed that, according to Swiss law, it would not be possible for him to receive the records because they were part of the confidential personnel file of each employee. As noted, such detailed requests tend to be refused by some and not others, and usually if investors are perceived as being too minor they might be refused evidence of the past experience of the manager's team. I still think it is worth the effort to acquire what you need to check such detail. I like to check randomly that degrees that are referred to are indeed held. The same goes for Certified Financial Analyst (CFA) or other professional qualifications, which are usually easily accessible from the relevant bodies that issue the qualification.

Difficulty in identifying the right individual

When you do a background check, be aware that you may encounter certain difficulties when researching certain individuals. It is easy to mistakenly search the wrong person as some individuals have the same name, even within the fund industry! Gather as much information as possible on the person first, for example, full name, date of birth, educational records, etc. That way you can quickly determine if you are on the right track. If you don't, the risk is that you might only discover this after hours of work!

How long will it take?

Although you hope to obtain information instantly, when you perform a background check, it may take time. Do not forget that some verifications in themselves will require that someone else has to come back to you. This is the case, for example, in connection with a professional degree verification from the Certified Alternative Investment Analyst Association (CAIA), which will take 24 hours to receive. Other institutions may take several days to get back to you, for example, upon written request the CFA will take three to five business days to verify an individual's CFA credentials; however, permission from the individual is required as well.

Practical steps

Considering the guidelines above, I think that a good, free way to go about doing a background check is to follow the five steps below.

Step 1: Google, KYC360 and other general level searches

A basic check on an internet search engine such as Google may provide very useful preliminary information on the individuals working for the fund and the manager or any other financial services company. In addition, a website that I find particularly helpful is KYC360, an online anti-money laundering community: **www.kyc360.com**.

KYC360 enables you to type in an individual's name and the site will then find all the relevant news articles on this person. This is a targeted search and therefore generally tends to be more refined than a general Google search. KYC360 is free and all you have to do in order to access its targeted search is to log in as a new member.

In addition you should check for any reported litigation on any person you are reviewing. Such litigation searches are best done through legal or court databases. In relation to checking any potential key man risk, if a senior individual is facing litigation this could significantly increase the risk that the fund's performance and finances are in jeopardy (see Chapter 8 for key man risk). Owing to the time it takes, litigation would have an impact on any senior person, and hence potentially damage their role and focus.

Step 2: Regulatory level searches

Regulators may well be one of the most reliable sources for compliance reviews, so it is helpful to have a good look at regulators' websites (as listed in Chapter 9). To give you an example of what I mean and how relevant this is take the case of the German K1 Fund. It seems that many investors and/or other third parties to the fund failed to pick up on a fraud, yet the regulator held all the information needed to put anyone on alert. If I were an investor interested in the K1 Fund in 2003, I would have been concerned by the fact that K1 had received warnings and been the subject of prosecutions from the German regulator, BaFin, from as early as 2001. This information was freely available on BaFin's website.

The K1 Fund

In brief:

- Helmut Kiener founded the K1 Group in 1995 whilst still working as an advertising salesman.

- The K1 Group prospered through managing two hedge funds, K1 Global and K1 Invest, registered in the British Virgin Islands. The funds were mainly marketed to and invested in by German-based private investors. By 1999 Kiener claimed to have made €13 million for 100 investors.

- In 2001, the German regulator, BaFin, investigated the K1 Global and K1 Invest Funds and prohibited further investments in the funds. Despite BaFin having issued several warnings and prosecutions between 2001 and 2008, investigations showed that, for example, in 2006–08 the K1 Group had allegedly received a further €300 million in subscriptions.[2]

- Kiener claimed returns of 825 per cent between 1996 and the middle of 2008.

- Essentially the fraud involved the following:

  - Investors fell victim to a Ponzi scheme as Kiener diverted money through an international network of firms that he controlled, allowing him to send monies into, for example, real estate in Florida, while feeding funds back into his firm.

  - Two banks, Barclays Plc and BNP Paribas SA were tricked into making their investments with false account statements.[3] The banks lost a combined total of €223 million and private investors lost approximately €122 million in the scam.

  - Kiener admitted to having secretly violated agreements with banks on how to handle funds they entrusted to his operations.

- In October 2010, Kiener was arrested in connection with an investigation for fraud and breach of trust.

---

[2] http://www.enotes.com/topic/K1_fund

[3] http://www.bloomberg.com/news/2010-11-16/k1-hedge-fund-founder-kiener-charged-in-germany-over-barclays-bnp-losses.html; http://www.bloomberg.com/news/2011-04-13/k1-group-hedge-fund-s-kiener-to-testify-at-german-fraud-trial.html

▶

> ■ In April 2011, Kiener admitted that he had attempted to make up for
> losses with money from new investors.
>
> ■ German courts sentenced him to 10 years and eight months in
> prison for tax evasion, 10 counts of fraud and 86 counts of forgery.[4]
>
> **Lessons learned**
>
> ■ Look out for any previous regulatory records – Germany's financial
> regulator, BaFin, issued warnings against Kiener's fund several times
> between 2001 and 2008.
>
> ■ Be wary of lack of work experience – Kiener was a former
> psychologist and initially started the K1 Group as an advertising
> salesman.

Step 3: Company register level searches

Managers are usually companies incorporated in various well recognised
jurisdictions, each with their company registers giving access to publicly
available information. You should use this information and confirm the
type of company you are dealing with (whether a partnership or limited liability company), who the owners are (whether individuals whose
name you recognise or third parties) and to determine the sources of
influence and control. You can also check the board composition and
the annual financial statements in most jurisdictions. Simple checks like
these which cost very little will provide vital insights.

For example, in the case of the failed manager, Weavering Capital, the
publicly available company accounts indicated an incredibly high rent
for office space and high local expenditure in comparison to the relatively small size of the fund it operated. In this case, a quick look at
the company's accounts would have highlighted the possibility that
managers were under immense pressure to earn more and possibly
take more risk as a result. I remember treating this as one of many red
flags for the manager.

---

[4] http://www.telegraph.co.uk/finance/financial-crime/8655763/10-years-in-prison-
for-Germanys-Mini-Madoff.html

In my view, it is clear that a manager with a poor balance sheet or under pressure from losses will be under 'stress' and this may lead to it taking more risk. There is also the risk of breaching rules on regulatory capital requirements, which, of themselves, could lead to the regulator intervening.

I have found it very useful therefore to check the official websites of the company registers listed in Table 10.1. Note that some of these sites are not free although the majority are.

You can find a list of links to company registers for a broad range of countries using the website for Official Company Registers at: **http://www.rba.co.uk/sources/registers.htm**. Alternatively, you can do company register searches on specific countries' websites listed in Table 10.1. Note that the US does not have a company register website equivalent. In order to find listings of companies in the US, you will need to do a search into each specific state's records.

Table 10.1 Company register websites

Canada – Industry Canada Register; or Sedar website	**http://strategis.gc.ca/eic/site/cd-dgc.nsf/eng/cs01134.html** or **http://www.sedar.com/search/search_form_pc_en.htm**
France – Infogreffe or the National Council of Business Registrars and Commercial Courts	**http://www.infogreffe.fr/infogreffe/index.jsp** or **http://www.cngtc.fr/english.php**
Hong Kong – the Integrated Registered Companies Information	**http://www.icris.cr.gov.hk/csci/**
Ireland – SoloCheck	**http://solocheck.ie/welcome.jsp**
Luxembourg	**https://www.rcsl.lu**
Singapore – Accounting and Corporate Regulatory Authority	**http://www.acra.gov.sg/**
UK – Companies House	**http://wck2.companieshouse.gov.uk**

Step 4: Criminal record search

In addition to the general internet search and regulatory websites searches, it is useful to research whether the manager's staff has any criminal records. In order to do a criminal check, I suggest that you look into the courts and public records of the relevant jurisdiction(s) but as said before, there may be limitations with regards to the amount of information available. For example, a search into the US courts system is easily accessible and very comprehensive. However, you would not be able to find much public information on Japanese court rulings as this is not publicly available, and a criminal search in the UK is not possible without the relevant individual's consent.

Table 10.2 lists some useful websites to use when carrying out searches on criminal records.

Table 10.2 Criminal records websites

US	General search (not free):	**www.criminalsearches.com**
	US Courts Filing Review (not free):	Pacer: **https://pcl.uscourts.gov/login?appurl=https://pcl.uscourts.gov/search**
	US Personal and Drinking Under the Influence (DUI) Records (not free):	(i) Intelius: **https://www.intelius.com/**
		(ii) DUI Records: **http://duirecords.org/**
		(iii) The Work Number: **http://theworknumber.com/**
UK	Record of court sentences (registration required, free)	**www.thelawpages.com**

Apart from the above record of court sentences, in the UK full criminal records are not publicly available and cannot be viewed without the relevant person's consent. It would therefore be difficult to do such a search on a manager's staff. If you are able to obtain consent, criminal records in the UK can be found at:

■ **www.businesslink.gov.uk/crb** (England and Wales);

■ **www.disclosurescotland.co.uk** (Scotland); and

■ **www.dojni.gov.uk/accessni** (Northern Ireland).

Similarly in France, the French Ministry of Justice may issue criminal record certificates but only to the person concerned. This can be requested via its website: **www.cjn.justice.gouv.fr**

Step 5: Credit, professional and educational level search:

There are further searches that you can do (see Table 10.3) and all of them are invaluable as they could reveal some very relevant information.

Table 10.3 General searches

Chartered Alternative Investment Analyst (CAIA)	CAIA email: member@caia.org Or call: +1-413-253-7373
Chartered Financial Analyst (CFA)	CFA Directory: **http://www.cfainstitute.org/finsecustomer_enu/start.swe?SWECmd=GotoView&SWEView=CFA+PMD+Home+Page+View+%28eApps%29** Or call: +1-434-951-5499
Credit profile check for UK companies (not free)	**http://www.jordans.co.uk/businessinformation/ukcompanysearches.html**
Educational checks	National Student Clearing House (for US only): **http://studentclearinghouse.com/** In order to search the National Student Clearing House, you will require the individual's school name, degree subject name and date of birth.
UK bankruptcy records	(i) Bankruptcy register: **http://www.insolvency.gov.uk/bankruptcy/bankruptcysearch.htm** (ii) Experian (not free): **http://www.experian.co.uk/** (iii) Land registry: **http://www1.landregistry.gov.uk/assets/library/documents/k16.pdf**
US General Background check (not so reliable if middle name is not available)	Intelius: **https://www.intelius.com/**
US Public Records (free Government public record sites)	BRB Publications : **http://www.brbpub.com/freeresources/pubrecsites.aspx?h=1**

Summary

■ Background checks can be done by investors themselves using the internet and are not difficult to do.

■ There are five recommended search steps:

- Google, KYC360 and other general level searches;
- a regulatory level search;
- a company register level search;
- a criminal record search;
- a credit, professional and educational level search.

11

Conclusion

What topics are covered in this chapter?

- The value of due diligence
- The future of the fund industry's service providers and advisors to investors
- New regulation – what is it good for?

In October 2009 the *Financial Times* reported that trust in financial services had hit a low. It was said that, according to a survey done by Direct Marketing Association, just 7 per cent agreed with the statement 'In the current economic climate, I trust the financial services industry to look out for me', while 60 per cent disagreed!

There were similar negative feelings for rating agencies. Following criticism of their activities and processes after 2008 and again in 2011, notably in relation to government ratings, many investors do not know what to make of the value of their views. This comes at a time when many **managers** still use ratings for their **funds** as a marketing lure.

Further, many private banks, and funds of funds were also criticised for mishandling many aspects of the financial excesses that preceded the crisis of 2008 by, for example, either putting their clients in mortgage related products disguised as money market funds or, in the worst cases, choosing funds like the ones offered by Madoff without proper care.

Clearly the industry has a long way to go to make up for its failings. You may think therefore that I favour new regulation, but I do not. I have always felt that there was plenty of good regulation and guidance but that it was simply ignored and not enforced. I have read all the new regulations and my mind has not changed. The new regulations may improve things but do not actually resolve, in my view, some of the core issues; and worse some may hurt investors by limiting access to investment opportunities.

I also sympathise with investors who feel that they should be able to buy what they want and trust what they are told by managers, without government interference. This book illustrates many aspects of what investors might do to verify what is said to them, thus protecting this independence. I do not see that new regulations change the need for that verification process.

I think the industry will improve if its most important actors, the investors, demand a change. To do so it is important for all investors to require the same standard and be sufficiently aware of the fundamental issues regarding the industry to air their concerns with one common voice.

The value of due diligence

There is no doubt that at present, even in the worst cases, there is little that can be done to punish those responsible for the abuses of fraud or other negligence in the investment fund industry. Even in the case of Weavering Capital (discussed in full in Chapter 4) the UK's Serious Fraud Office dropped its investigation in 2011. This was terrible news for investors. From a legal point of view this reflects a concern that very often such cases are too hard to prosecute and leaves one with the feeling that there is no accountability for managers who abuse their rights, even in the UK's sacrosanct legal system. The structure of funds and managers is such that the liability is too remote for key principals who protect themselves through standard legal structures. This could be changed and to some degree has been addressed in the new legal regulations that are coming out.

From a practical point of view, however, this emphasises that the only solution for investors, based on the traditional *caveat emptor* principle, is that they have to watch out for themselves and do their own due diligence or work with people who do and that they can rely on. As long as investors are aware of the risks they will improve standards by choosing funds more carefully and in accordance with their own assessments of the relevant operational risks that they can judge quite generally. I hope this book provides the relevant insights for these assessments. It is not hard to check a few things that should put you on notice of potential problems, even if it takes time.

In fact I was surprised recently to find that even one of the most experienced investors, who had not done his due diligence carefully, was caught up in problems. This goes to show that as soon as you invest in any company that is not listed, and that is similar, as I have explained in this book, to you investing indirectly in the manager of your chosen fund, then you have to invest time in reviewing its operations.

---

case study   Fidelity China Special Situations Fund

In brief:

- Fidelity China Special Situations Fund (the 'fund') is managed by Fidelity China Special Situations PLC ('Fidelity'), an investment trust listed on the London Stock Exchange.

- Fidelity is run by one of the UK's best known asset managers, Anthony Bolton.

- The fund was launched in April 2010 and raised £460 million during the initial public offering.

- In July 2011, Bolton liquidated its holdings in several Chinese reverse merger stocks at a loss, two of which were small US-listed Chinese companies accused of fraud.

- Bolton confirmed that the losses only represented a small percentage of the overall portfolio of the fund.

- Bolton affirmed that he will now enforce stronger due diligence before making investment decisions for the fund.

▶

I have chosen the Fidelity China Special Situations fund to illustrate that even the best asset managers in the world can be invested in fraudulent companies if a comprehensive due diligence check is not carried out beforehand.

Bolton, the asset manager, had previously managed the Fidelity Special Situations Fund from December 1979 to December 2007. Over the 28-year period in which Bolton ran the Special Situations Fund, he successfully led the fund to achieve annualised growth of 19.5 per cent, far in excess of the 13.5 per cent growth of the wider stock exchange. After a two-year break, Bolton announced his return in 2009 and in April 2010 he moved to Hong Kong to run his new Fidelity China Special Situations Fund. The fund raised £460 million when it launched in April 2010.

In July 2011, Bolton revealed that the fund had liquidated its holdings in several Chinese reverse merger stocks at a loss, two of which were small US-listed Chinese companies accused of fraud. He said in an interview with the *Financial Times* that he had underestimated the risk of investing in China and that, as a result, he was now going to spend more time on due diligence.[1] One of the Chinese companies, China Integrated Energy, lost 90 per cent of its market value in 2011 after its alleged involvement in fraud. The company's **auditor**, KPMG, resigned following the fraud accusation; however the company has denied any wrong-doing and has launched an independent investigation into the accusation. Bolton did not name the other Chinese company or the extent of losses that his fund had suffered.

The problem with going on about due diligence is that it may leave a feeling that you have to redo the job of your **advisors**. This is up to you, and there are many types of advisors. There is unfortunately such a low threshold of competence in so many financial institutions that this approach may still save you lots of money. Some of the new laws and regulations could bring about an improvement to standards and this may lessen the need for due diligence in years to come, but not yet.

---

[1] http://www.telegraph.co.uk/finance/personalfinance/investing/8639266/Anthony-Boltons-China-fund-hit-by-fraud-losses.html

It is also worth noting the view of Steven Brown, Professor of Finance at New York University on this. In an interview on Opalesque TV in February 2012, he noted that operational due diligence should feature as a form of 'alpha creation' and that costs for independent due diligence should be about $15,000 which is not so expensive for the value he deems it will add to fund selection.[2]

The future of the fund industry's service providers and advisors to investors

In the meantime the big question is: who can an investor trust? This concerns all of the actors involved in the financial industry, from large banks to smaller institutions, rating agencies to consultants, advisors and managers. Many of these financial leaders, including some very good ones, got caught up with the wave of failure that stigmatised the 2008 crisis by not thoroughly checking their facts and not doing their jobs properly. In the end that led to direct or indirect misrepresentations. It also led very often to ignoring the best interest of investors. What made things worse is that, for the most part, losses were borne by the investors but not their professional bankers or managers who in the end either kept what had been earned already or if not, nonetheless benefited from the governments' bail outs paid for by the taxpayer.

Fund service providers

Service providers will find it hard to justify the reliability of their work in the years ahead unless some fundamental issues are addressed and standards unified globally. There are still too many conflicts in the financial industry in the way it operates to make the provision of services impartial. The desire to see investors being better protected has been the catalyst behind much government action world-wide for many years, but a lack of practical understanding and a desire to limit costs on the industry has meant that some important opportunities to improve standards may have been missed. What is happening following 2008 is that we are seeing a shift from the trust that bound financial advisors and bankers with their clients, to the less personal but perhaps more

[2] http://www.opalesque.tv/hedge-fund-videos/Stephen_Brown/1

reliable government backed UCITS or equivalent fund set up which is now trumpeted as a standard for investor protection.

As discussed in Chapter 5, however, I do not think enough is done to secure the role of the independent third party **administrators** even in EU regulated **UCITS**. This would have been essential to ensure fair pricing, especially where funds use hard-to-value assets and this includes some of the derivatives used by UCITS. The need for independence grows in my view with the complexity of the underlying investments.

Ideally, as part of the financial industry's processes, with the backing of a stronger legal framework, the administrator should be working with the manager to set standards when dealing with the valuation of hard-to-value assets. This process should be fully disclosed to the public, with the ability to verify it by accessing existing records proving that the valuation process is followed. There has been an increasing trend for institutional investors to request internal pricing policies, especially for level 2 and level 3 types of instruments. However on this point, new laws have not been very effective.

In a similar vein, although **custodians** are also part of the complex new regulations, in Europe at least, it is not clear what their role is in verifying the existence of assets. Many banks work with other banks and traditionally the ownership of assets is not always clearly prescribed in legal form. This has left an industry behind the times, where electronic trading and reconciliation systems are often too complex to be properly implemented and followed. Again, this is an area that is hard to penetrate for any regulator, and most have instead targeted the need for a higher capital base in financial institutions that control client money and assets.

Consultants

Consultancy firms have been an active provider of services to investors, traditionally acting in connection with pension funds but also more and more with other financial institutions. Their role is very varied, but generally it is to advise their clients on how they should invest their money in relation to their global holdings and to meet potential future liabilities. For example, they might provide a list of preferred funds that they deem to be good for returns in the context of the client's global holdings. This is usually still based on traditional financial analysis and performance results. More and more consultants, however, now appreciate the importance of linking their advice to operational reviews, especially after many were criticised by their client base for taking them into liability mismatch territory or for exposing them to fraudulent managers. Cases against consultants following the 2008 crisis are many, especially in the US, and include a Milwaukee County claim for $100 million, a claim by Kentucky Fried Chicken for £15 million and a claim by Kern County Employees' Retirement Association for $4 million. This last claim was in relation to an investment in Westridge Capital Management (see the case below).

I think that consultants play a big role in the industry and certainly provide valuable if not the only assistance to many people with their investment choices. Having said that I am concerned that they have a monopoly, at least in the UK, over guiding the choices of pension funds and in my view have not adapted fast enough to the developing fund industry that now offers complex alternative products. In fact, consultants have not yet proven that they have the means to verify operations and related risks of operational failure and fraud. In terms of conflict of interests there are also issues where, as shown in the case that follows, sometimes consultants can be paid by the product provider as well as the investor they advise.

case study   WG Trading

In brief:

▨ In 1979 Stephen Walsh and Paul Greenwood founded the WG Trading Company, along with two affiliated entities: Westridge Capital Management and WG Investors.

▨ From 1996 to February 2009 Walsh and Greenwood misappropriated $553 million of $1.3 billion in funds from commodity pool investors.

▨ Walsh and Greenwood allegedly had close ties with a number of prominent consulting firms. These consulting firms highly recommended WG Trading to large institutional investors, including several public pension funds, educational institutions and endowments in the US.

▶

▶

Walsh and Greenwood told investors that their money was going to be placed in a stock index arbitrage strategy.

■ Instead, the two managers used investor money to cover personal expenses and prior losses, and bought luxury cars, multimillion dollar residences, expensive art and so on.

■ The SEC and the **CFTC** charged Walsh and Greenwood with conspiracy, securities fraud, wire fraud and money laundering.

■ On 25 February 2009 Walsh and Greenwood were arrested and bail was set at $7 million each.

■ On 28 July 2010 Greenwood pleaded guilty to criminal violations and agreed to testify against Walsh. Greenwood is permanently barred from trading commodity futures and options contracts, soliciting funds for trading and registering with the CFTC. He will also have to surrender ill-gotten gains to defrauded investors and pay a civil monetary penalty.

■ The criminal and civil cases against Walsh continue.

Lessons learned

■ Consultancy firms may promote certain funds to investors based on personal ties or connections.

■ Consultants may have commissions which give them an interest in promoting a fund.

■ Not all consultants understand the risks associated with some complex strategies that fall outside of their traditional expertise which is in accounting and assets and liabilities mis-match, not in fund management operations. Here notably you should have expected and seen much higher standards of due diligence exercised by consultants.

Rating agencies

At present the rating agencies are obviously suffering with many reports putting in doubt the viability of a rating. Many investors are used to relying on rating agencies as they have historically been relevant in rating corporate issues and government securities. Their popularity and relevance was undiminished until 2008 which exposed for many of them the poorly thought out processes which led them to provide ratings for certain funds and financial institutions that then failed. Unfortunately, the rating agencies followed their classic model of being paid by the issuer of the rated product, including the fund. This creates an immediate conflict of interest in my view which is not reconcilable with the needs of the industry. Further, rating agencies only started rating funds in recent years and seem to have failed to appreciate that funds and managers are complex private operations that demand a lot of resources to review properly. This is not a quick process as we can see from this book. I am also not sure that many funds now view a rating as a useful aid for marketing purposes, as investors hardly seem to rely on them at all.

Since the 2008 financial crisis, the relationship of trust between investors and credit rating agencies may indeed be beyond repair and ratings even by names such as Moody's or Standard & Poor's (S&P) are regarded with more caution. Credit rating agencies in particular were placed at the centre of the US sub-prime mortgage crisis owing to the fact that they over-rated complex financial products that were based on largely worthless mortgages. Since the agencies gave good ratings to such products, banks bought risky debts (without doing their own checks) that they may not normally have backed. Accordingly, Joseph Stiglitz, a Nobel prize-winning economist, labelled rating agencies as one of the 'key culprits' of the financial crisis. I do not agree with this label but some review of their own operations is clearly required.

The *Guardian* newspaper developed the notion of the inherent conflict of interest, which it argued the credit rating agencies suffered from, in an article published on 22 August 2011. In this same article the former senior president at Moody's, William Harrington, was reported to have attacked credit rating agencies for being 'paid by banks and companies that they are supposed to rate objectively'. He revealed that this 'salient conflict of interest permeates all levels of employment, from entry-level analyst to the chairman and chief executive officer of Moody's corporation'. Furthermore, Harrington warns us that, whilst the SEC in the US is considering new rules to reform the agencies, this will do 'little to improve the situation and could make it easier for agencies to pressure their staff'. I tend to have sympathy with that view. Unless you can separate the economic interest from the assessment, it will always have a bearing on what is written up by the rating agency.

For example, Moody's rating of the bank Bear Stearns was ongoing even when it was bailing out its funds, although this is not to say it was linked to any conflicts of interest, it was a notable mistake:

Moody's rating of Bear Stearns Companies Inc

Moody's rated Bear Stearns in 2007 as it was allegedly injecting assets into its money losing High-Grade Structured Credit Fund.

It was apparently the case that Moody's was impressed by Bear Stearns, which was noted to have maintained a high rating of A1/ Prime 1 because it was deemed careful when managing its risk. Moody's was particularly impressed by the risk management aspect and this was raised as evidence of Bear Stearns' stability by Moody's Senior Vice President at the time, Blaine Frantz. There was a genuine conviction that Bear Stearns had the required liquidity and sufficient levels of credit available should anything go against the firm, even if the changes to the mortgage business were already palpable.

Now of course in ratings nothing is a perfect science. With regards to funds two rating agencies, including industry specialists Amber Partners, certified certain funds managed by Bear Stearns Asset Management before they failed. Other funds that were rated before failing include Vega Asset Management. Both Bear Stearns Asset Management[3] and Vega Asset Management[4] had funds that blew up in relation to the application of their investment strategy and probable lack of risk controls. Whether that was missed or was not relevant when the rating was done is impossible to say but it could also be somehow related to the same issues that have plagued the rating of debt instruments.

[3] http://www.sec.gov/news/press/2008/2008-115.htm

[4] http://www.realcrash.com/hedge-fund-s-m/2/; http://dealbreaker.com/_old/images/entries/Vega_Letter.pdf

I think it is safe to say that the whole financial industry would benefit from clearer controls over conflicts of interests, especially for any firm that is supposed to reveal the failures of its clients to the outside world. Rating agencies reached their limits during the 2008 financial crisis. Perhaps it is time for the regulator to assume greater control over rating agencies as happened in Australia? I do not believe that in the end regulation in itself will be sufficient; otherwise our banks which are heavily regulated would not have failed us too. What is needed is a more prescriptive approach to regulation where necessary and many more actual and practical controls.

New regulation – what is it good for?

In the end, following 2008, what investors will inherit is a lot of new legislation, the costs of which will probably be passed on to them. The regulations may not be as focused or relevant as they need to be and therefore could prove punitive on the financial industry which we all rely on so much for our pensions. I have always maintained that in many regards the existing regulatory framework present before 2008 was sufficient in theory, but it was not enforced. If only it had been properly implemented and had the backing of proper enforcement, it would have stopped a lot of abuses. This view is supported by the recent case of Mercurius Capital, which shows that under the existing UK framework (pre-UCITS IV or AIFMD) the FSA is perfectly capable of enforcing a good standard, albeit after the event, but at least the standard is there.

---

case study   Mercurius Capital Management Limited

- Cayman Island based Mercurius International Fund Limited launched in early 2003.

- Mercurius Capital Management Limited ('Mercurius') acted as manager for the fund, led by CEO Michiel Visser and CFO Oluwole Modupe Fagbulu.

▶

■ The fund allegedly invested in three main strategies: 1) selecting underperforming stocks; 2) short-term trends, high-volume trading; and 3) event driven stock selection based on corporate events such as mergers, acquisitions and initial public offerings (IPOs).

■ The fund performed well for its first three years from 2003 to 2006.

■ By mid-2006, the fund's performance dropped. The fund had apparently invested too heavily in NT Energy, an unlisted company, which had shares that decreased in value. Despite this, Visser continued to invest more in NT Energy, going beyond the fund's investment restrictions.

■ The fund struggled with the resignation of two **prime brokers** in 2007.

■ The fund collapsed and went into voluntary liquidation in January 2008.

■ The FSA found both Visser and Fagbulu guilty of market manipulation, breach of investment restrictions and misleading investors. In March 2010[5] both men were banned from the financial services industry and received fines:

   – Fagbulu received a penalty of £500,000.

   – Visser was charged £2 million, the largest fine given to an asset manager to date by the FSA.[6]

■ Fagbulu and Visser appealed to the Upper Tribunal against the FSA's decision: however this was upheld by the tribunal in August 2011 with the exception of Fagbulu's fine which was reduced to £100,000.[7]

Mercurius was a UK company authorised by the FSA to act as manager for a hedge fund based in the Cayman Islands, Mercurius International Fund Limited (the 'fund'). Although this fund is not one of the largest frauds or failures out there, I think it is a significant example as it represents the biggest fine the UK's FSA has given to any asset manager for market manipulation and misleading investors. Further,

---

[5] http://www.fsa.gov.uk/pubs/final/michiel_visser.pdf

[6] http://www.tribunals.gov.uk/financeandtax/Documents/decisions/VisserandFagbulu_v_FSA.pdf

[7] http://www.tribunals.gov.uk/financeandtax/documents/decisions/visserandfagbulu_v_fsa.pdf; http://www.allenovery.com/AOWEB/AreasOfExpertise/Editorial.aspx?contentTypeID=1&itemID=64131&prefLangID=410

it shows just how easily individuals can manipulate the market, breach investment restrictions and mislead investors, but more tellingly are caught and forbidden to trade under current regulations and laws.

Dutch asset manager Michiel Visser was the CEO and sole director of Mercurius and was the primary person responsible for running the fund and making investment decisions. Visser launched Mercurius in 2002 after holding senior positions at ABN Amro Asset Management. The fund was launched in early 2003 and approximately six months later Visser employed Oluwole Modupe Fagbulu to act as CFO as well as to take on the role of **compliance** oversight.

- During its five year life-span the fund had on average 20 main investors with approximately $35 million in **AUM**. The fund's three main investment strategies were: first, a fundamental stock pricing strategy, which selected stocks that were underperforming in the market;

- second, a directional strategy, which used short-term, high-volume trading in order to profit from short-term trends; and

- third, an event-driven strategy, which took positions on corporate events such as mergers, acquisitions and IPOs.

The fund's first three years between 2003 and 2006 were a success, however by the summer of 2006 the fund was not performing well. In March of the same year the fund made its first investment in NT Energy, an unlisted company that develops oil leases in Texas. This bad investment decision led to the eventual collapse of the fund. The fund initially bought 1.5 million shares in NT Energy at a cost of £3 million, in anticipation of an IPO potentially for September 2006. However, NT Energy delayed its IPO, allegedly seeking to raise capital elsewhere. Despite this, Visser continued to invest first in NT Energy and then in Sandhaven, a listed company that had, itself, invested in NT Energy.

A reduction in the value of the fund's portfolio between December 2006 and February 2007 meant that when the fund sold some of its assets, the value of the fund's holding in NT Energy ended up being in excess of its 30 per cent investment limit. Over the next 10 months, Visser apparently kept buying into NT Energy such that by the end of February 2007, the fund had a reported 43.8 per cent of its assets invested in NT Energy shares, which were illiquid assets.

In August 2006, one of Mercurius' investors, a German bank called Sal Oppenheim, had asked for a **side letter** from Attica Capital, one of its investment management companies, which passed on the request to Visser. This side letter included a restriction which limited any investment in unlisted companies to 30 per cent of the fund's assets. Visser signed the letter and returned it to Attica Capital. Despite this neither Attica Capital nor Sal Oppenheim were informed of the breach that had taken place. They invested an additional $1.18 million in Mercurius between November and December 2006.

The fund's downfall was further affected when BNP Paribas, the fund's prime broker, gave notice that it would be terminating its relationship with the fund in January 2007. The prime broker's resignation put Visser in a sudden funding crisis as it meant that the fund could no longer make margin trades. It was by then increasingly reliant on such trades given its recent poor performance. Whilst searching for a new prime broker, the manager of the fund apparently undertook two fictitious transactions which the FSA says were secured loans at extremely high interest rates, disguised as share sales. Mercurius' position then worsened when its second prime broker, Citi Prime Services, resigned after only six months.

The fund collapsed and was placed in voluntary liquidation in January 2008. Investors have not recovered their money, and it appears unlikely that they ever will.

It was discovered that both Visser and Fagbulu deliberately concealed the deterioration in the fund's performance from investors as they wanted new investors to put money into the fund and did not want existing investors to ask for redemptions. Such concealment of the fund's true performance meant that Mercurius succeeded in attracting €8 million in new investments between late September 2007 and the fund's collapse in early 2008.

In March 2011, after an investigation into Visser and Fagbulu's actions, the FSA found both men guilty of four FSA violations:

1 disregard of investment restrictions and limits set out in the **prospectus**;

2 deliberate market manipulation;

3 falsely enhancing the fund's **NAV** by entering into fictitious transactions; and

4 issuing misleading investor communications – which led investors to believe the fund was doing well when, in fact, it was not – as well as deliberately failing to inform investors of important developments such as the resignation of two of its prime brokers.

The FSA withdrew Visser's and Fagbulu's FSA approvals as authorised individuals and banned both men from any future involvement in the financial services industry. Further, a financial penalty was imposed on Fagbulu for £500,000 for his role in approving communication to investors which he knew contained false information and for failing to ensure that the fund complied with investment restrictions. His fine was, however, reduced to £100,000 on the basis of financial hardship.

Visser's fine has been set at £2 million for breach of the FSA's principle of integrity and for engaging in market abuse. Visser failed to appear before the Tax and Chancery Chamber of the Upper Tribunal in March 2011 which upheld the FSA's £2 million levy, calling the CEO's actions 'worse than any other seen by this tribunal'.

Although the decision against Visser is subject to appeal, I think the developments in this case are good news for investors. It means that managers are being held accountable for their actions and fined accordingly. It also means that any officer, notably those with compliance responsibilities (CF10), even when not acting as directors, as was the case for Fagbulu, face a real liability for the actions of their manager. This hopefully will continue to show that taking compliance seriously is the only way to maintain a quality asset management business. Those with CF10 responsibilities must have enough resources to do their job and work with the right professionals if they alone cannot meet their responsibilities. Fagbulu was also the financial officer, and the two jobs are in their own right extremely onerous, very different and clearly potentially conflicted.

Further, the Tribunal's decision emphasises the need for due diligence. Mercurius, whilst heading for failure, was still able to raise €8 million of assets from September 2007. Investors could have avoided this by effecting simple but proper due diligence checks on the fund and manager.

Finally, the Tribunal also noted the restrictions in the prospectus which means that they will count, at least within the UK, even if the fund is not on shore.

Lessons learned

1 Consider whether the fund's strategy represents a high-risk investment.

   ▨ Investors of Mercurius' fund should certainly have been aware that the fund represented a high-investment risk, with the prospect of large gains but also the possibility of losses notably in unlisted securities which are also a hard to value asset.

2 Do your own check on the status of service providers.

   ▨ Investors should have been able to pick up warning signs easily, such as the prime brokers of the fund having resigned whilst being represented as still acting for the fund.

   ▨ The first prime broker was BNP Paribas, which had resigned by February 2007, and then Citigroup Global Markets, which resigned by September 2007.

   ▨ Despite that, investors who did not seek references from the named prime brokers continued to invest.

3 Be wary of individuals in the manager who hold many positions of responsibility.

   ▨ Fagbulu held the positions of CFO and compliance officer.

   ▨ These two roles are very different and both are onerous. You should question whether the individual has the capacity and necessary skills to effectively carry out each role in the manager.

   ▨ Also think of conflicts, as compliance should be independent of all other business roles.

Nevertheless the regulatory framework has changed much since 2008, if only because of UCITS IV and AIFMD in Europe. There has also been an interest in more regulated products, notably under the form of ETFs and index tracking funds, especially if they can qualify as UCITS.

UCITS

It is questionable whether an investment strategy that carries the UCITS label is safer than any other, but at least the funds have limitations on what they can do. Those limitations, although beneficial from a legal point of view, may be harmful from an economic point of view as they may reduce the potential for actual performance.

Remember that UCITS IV was under way well before the 2008 crisis but its implementation was much influenced by those events. UCITS funds also include ETFs and index tracking funds (allowed under UCITS III already). All these products were designed to assist with the convergence of European funds. Now the UCITS IV directive has added many new rules regarding risk management, notably by the manager (as opposed to the fund) and in some cases by the service providers of the funds (the administrator and custodian).

Some parts of the law are focusing on the responsibilities of the custodian. There was a perception that with Madoff, too many custodians were just happy to accept what was being said to them in relation to assets held in various accounts, without formally checking, and the regulator is looking at clearly delineating what responsibilities a custodian should have. It will be interesting to see what happens as a result. I think it is unlikely to change enough aspects, as the valuation of the asset is still the key problem and this is not addressed by the directives. In the meantime, custodians are very concerned about their ability to continue offering their services at relatively competitive prices without incurring too many new liabilities. You can find a free booklet written about UCITS on the Laven Partners' website: **http://lavenpartners.com**.

AIFMD

In Europe the wind of change was blowing fast after 2008 which led to the birth of the AIFMD. Although designed to better control **offshore** funds and unregulated funds in Europe, it is currently incredibly hard to gauge the impact of this directive. It was born out of the idea that alternative funds were responsible for the 2008 crisis, which is nonsense and therefore probably not a good foundation. As it is, this directive will at best improve risk management, by creating some new and repeating some old requirements as to what managers must do. It will reiterate with some emphasis the onus on managers to control their funds' risks wherever they are situated. At worst this directive will reduce the access for European investors to the alternative industry at a time when this industry needs to perform for the sake of our pension funds.

AIFMD impact on investments

The article below, although a bit dated, summarises the issues with the AIFMD very well. It is a concern for all investors if in the end the directive fails to reach its goals.

Pension funds fear EU hedge funds rules

By Martin Arnold, 13 January 2010, *Financial Times*

Dutch pension funds have warned that proposed European Union regulation of hedge funds and private equity would cost them €1.5bn a year, adding to increasingly vocal criticism of the draft law from investors across Europe.

In a strongly-worded letter to the European Parliament's Committee on Economic and Monetary Affairs, 10 of the biggest Dutch pension funds with €500bn of assets said the proposed EU law would 'have an undue negative impact' on their industry.

They said that in its current form the draft EU law would force them to increase the contributions of their 7m pensioners by at least 6 per cent to cover the extra costs of the regulation and the lost income from having to move out of most non-EU funds.

'The ultimate effect of the proposal is that it still leads to an undue restriction of investment opportunities, higher costs and lower returns for investors,' they said.

Signatories to the letter included APG, manager of ABP, the third-largest pension fund in the world; PGGM, the Dutch healthcare fund; and the Shell and Unilever staff pension funds.

They proposed seven amendments to the draft law, which is being debated this month by the European Parliament. The most striking proposal was for a 'grand-fathering provision' that would exempt any investments made in funds based outside the EU before the law comes into force.

The move is the latest sign that investors are responding to calls from the private equity and hedge fund industries for them to speak out against the draft EU law on managers.

Germany's institutional funds industry recently criticised the draft law, arguing that it would damage the country's Spezialfonds, a domestic fund aimed only at institutional investors with about €690bn under management.

Several big UK investors have criticised the draft law. The investment chief of the Wellcome Trust, the UK's biggest charity, told the *Financial Times* last month that its financial performance would be hurt if the law was not changed.

The Dutch pension funds called for an exemption on the administration and servicing companies that many of them have set up to pool resources and manage their investments, which could otherwise be caught by the new law.

They also said that many of the EU's proposals were duplicating rules for other managers under MiFID and UCITS, which they said could be used to apply for hedge funds and private equity.

In addition, they called for a loosening of the proposed restrictions on access for EU investors to alternative investment funds based outside the EU. For example, they suggested allowing managers of non-EU funds to voluntarily submit to the new law in return for being authorised to raise money from EU investors.

They calculated the €1.5bn figure for losses on the basis that they would be forced to switch the 8.9 per cent of their €693bn portfolio that is invested in non-EU based alternative investment funds into less attractive assets, such as equities and bonds.

Summary

In this final chapter we discussed:

- the ongoing importance of due diligence for every investor;
- the future of the fund industry's service providers; and
- the impact of new regulations.

Glossary

Administrator The administrator is an independent third party that provides independent valuation for the underlying positions in the fund portfolio. The administrator provides the NAV calculations for investors. They can and often take on other responsibilities such as investor reporting, acting as the fund's registrar and sometimes procuring a director on the fund's board.

Advisor If a manager is offshore it may delegate advisory and or managerial services to another company which is called an advisor or sub-manager. This company is usually called an 'advisor' despite advisors having various functions and responsibilities and it is usually based in a major financial centre such as the UK or US.

Assets under management (AUM) AUM is the market value of assets that an investment company manages on behalf of its investors. For funds, the AUM reflects the size of the fund. AUM fluctuates according to the growth and/or decline in capital appreciation and the fund's money inflow and outflow.

Auditor The auditor provides a yearly review of the fund's accounts, and presents an independent opinion as to their validity. The audits of funds are deemed essential, as they are supposed to capture and provide a true representation of the underlying positions contained in the fund.

Background checks A background check is the process of searching and compiling the criminal records, employment records and financial records of the key persons involved in the fund or the manager. Some investors might be uncomfortable with investing with managers that have any disciplinary records, whereas others might ignore some details such as driving under the influence of alcohol or a bad debt history. Either way this information is deemed important and revealing about the character of those involved.

Board of directors The board is made up of a group of individuals that are selected to act on behalf of the fund or the manager (assuming they are both companies and not partnerships which are managed differently) to execute decisions on investment management and other issues. The quality and background of the board of directors should reflect the quality of the corporate governance. Some funds select experienced individuals who can be influential and independent whilst others will appoint so-called 'Mickey Mouse' directors, who simply execute the decisions made by the manager. The board of managers is usually more as one would expect as it includes members of the manager (usually the founding members/owners of the business).

Broker A broker is an independent agent, usually a bank, that arranges transactions between a buyer and a seller and gets a commission when deals are completed. A broker is an essential service provider to a fund because it makes the sale or purchase of securities on behalf of the fund. *Also see Prime Broker.*

Co-mingled account A co-mingled account is an account which holds assets from several account holders. Those assets are pooled together. Funds sometimes end up in co-mingled accounts as their banks use this to reduce costs. The downside for investors is that since the fund's money is combined with that of other investors, if any investor makes a loss or the bank goes into liquidation, it is difficult to determine how to separate out the assets from the co-mingled pool, especially if it is cash.

Commodity Futures Trading Commission (CFTC) The CFTC is an independent agency with the mandate to regulate the commodities futures and option markets in the US. The CFTC works closely with the NFA. The CFTC differs from the NFA as it deals exclusively with commodities futures, whereas the NFA covers the entire futures industry.

Commodity trading advisor (CTA) A CTA is an asset manager or firm that generally follows a set of systematic investment strategies in order to give people advice on options, futures and the trading of managed futures accounts. Such systematic investment strategies are based on fluctuations in computerised calculations and can be based on either short-term or long-term trends in the market. CTAs originally operated mainly in the commodities markets, however today they invest in any liquid futures market.

Compliance This reflects a manager's ability to comply with relevant regulations. It is significant as it is an indicator of whether the business itself is well managed. It is important to ensure that the manager is following all the relevant rules and regulations, has proper processes and controls in place, as well as that employees are properly trained and aware of existing regulations. This is all usually scripted by regulators so investors need only cross check that the script is adhered to and respected.

Contamination *See Cross liability.*

Controller A controller is a person that exercises any form of influence or direct control on a company. This is usually done by holding voting shares and thus shareholders are often referred to as controllers. Controllers can have a significant impact on the actions of the fund or the manager/advisor and may also be subject to conflicts of interests, for example, where the ownership of the fund is in the same hands as that of the manager.

Cross liability A fund that links investors by using different share classes within the same fund for different types of risk exposure, will put all those underlying investors at risk together. Indeed from a legal point of view no difference will be made amongst the share classes of one fund if any one is liquidated. Recourse may be had therefore on any of the assets of the other share classes. This is referred to as 'cross-liability' or 'contamination'.

Custodian *see Prime broker*

Due diligence questionnaire (DDQ) A DDQ is a checklist of questions concerning the main features of a fund, including its strategy, performance, personnel, risk management policies, etc. Once the manager provides answers to the questions in the DDQ, the investor should then have a clear understanding and overview of the strengths and weaknesses of the fund and/or its manager. It is very similar to a request for proposal, a term often used for regulated funds.

Financial Services Authority (FSA) The FSA is the regulator of all providers of financial services in the UK.

Fund The fund is a legal entity the main purpose of which is to allow investors to put their money into one pot which can grow free of tax. The fund can be formed in various ways such as a unit trust or a private company including using the partnership form. The most common form of fund for alternative funds is that of an offshore company usually with limited liability.

Gate Funds may have the right to raise a 'gate', which means that where a fund receives redemption requests within a redemption period exceeding a certain percentage of the NAV, it may delay the latest redemption requests until the next redemption period. Whether the fund has gates will be clear from the prospectus. In essence this is like chosing who can jump from the (usually) sinking ship and at what rate. If the gate is raised then you have to wait your turn.

High water mark The highest NAV of the previous financial year which the fund needs to reach before a performance fee becomes payable.

Hurdle rate The minimum agreed return which the fund needs to generate before a performance fee becomes payable. The hurdle rate can often be linked to a benchmark such as a hedge fund index.

Information ratio This is a measure that offers a simple and pragmatic way to determine the manager's ability to generate returns for a given level of risk. It calculates the expected active return of a fund's portfolio and divides it by the amount of risk for the same portfolio as measured by volatility. The higher the ratio, the better the manager is.

Internal Capital Adequacy Assessment Process (ICAAP) ICAAP is a regulatory requirement in Europe which requires that the management of a manager reviews the company's strategic and ongoing decision-making processes around risk and if need be increases its capital to cover for such risk. The ICAAP is used to show how much capital the manager should set aside to make sure that it has enough internal reserves to deal with operational risks. As part of the ICAAP a manager is required to prepare Pillar I, Pillar II and Pillar III reports and make public disclosures accordingly.

Investment advisory agreement This is an agreement between the manager and an investment advisor. It will set out the contractual terms binding on the advisor and usually either fully delegates largely similar responsibilities to those delegated to the manager or indeed it may seek to limit the delegation to certain areas of expertise. Some of the agreements are quite confusing as they are not always clearly negotiated since the parties tend to be related or affiliated and their purpose can at times be opaque.

Investment management agreement This is a contractual agreement between those who have money to invest (which could be a fund) and a manager. It sets out the terms and conditions applying to how assets will be looked after and which party has responsibility for certain obligations. The investment management agreement is most common between a fund and a manager and this reflects the delegation which is part of the common structure of funds.

Legal advisor Managers usually hire legal advisors on behalf of the fund to assist them in relation to fund matters. For alternative funds, the onshore counsel, for example in London and New York, is hired to do most of the work and draft the legal documents such as the prospectus, the investment management and investment advisory agreements. The offshore legal advisor helps to review that they are in line with the laws that apply to the fund's jurisdiction. The legal advisor is supposed to act in the fund's interests not those of investors. There is usually a tendency for the manager to have undue influence on the process of legal work which is not appreciated by investors who do not tend to have their own legal counsel other than in private equity funds.

Leverage Leverage is the degree of borrowing in a fund's strategy. The higher the degree of borrowing, the greater the fund's exposure to any risk of loss. The leverage used in any strategy is therefore relevant to its success as well as its demise.

Manager The management company or 'manager' of a fund is a corporate entity that is responsibile for investing the money that investors put into a fund. Performance of a fund is dependent on whether the manager's team is solid and well organised and whether the staff and principals of the management entity act in accordance with what is in the best interest of the fund and thus the investors.

Net Asset Value (NAV) The NAV shows the value of the fund's assets. It is the monetary value of a single fund share, based on the value of the underlying assets of the fund minus its liabilities, divided by the number of shares outstanding. The value of the assets is generally taken as the market price or book value. Asset valuation can be a complex exercise as soon as there is no market. The NAV is calculated at regular intervals depending on the liquidity of the fund. More frequent calculations will mean more costs for the fund and investors. With UCITS, the NAV is calculated more frequently (no later than every two weeks) as part of the legal framework. Other funds can do as they wish.

NFA (National Futures Association) The National Futures Association (NFA) is an independent, self-regulated organisation for the US futures industry. The purpose of the NFA is to safeguard market integrity, protect investors and help its members meet their regulatory responsibilities. The NFA works closely with the CFTC.

Onshore and offshore The terms onshore and offshore can be a cause of confusion and are derived from the US. The US traditionally had funds based in the US, targeted at US investors, and these were labelled as 'onshore'. When early managers started to set up funds in territories outside of the US, to accommodate non-US investors, this became termed as 'offshore'. Although Europe adopts similar 'onshore' and 'offshore' terminology, such terms are not very useful because there are very few EU domiciled funds in the main financial centres (as there were no laws to accommodate such vehicles until quite recently, and even now hedge funds are not very popular in high tax jurisdictions such as France or Germany despite some very good legislation). In relation to the UK, there are no onshore structures as there are still no laws to support them (although this may change soon); hence non-regulated alternative funds are offshore. Accordingly, an onshore management company usually refers to a manager based and incorporated in the UK.

Personal account dealing Some managers of funds allow their staff to trade for their personal account. There are rules however that prohibit this if it is done with private knowledge and for the purpose of illegitimate gain. Internally managers require that their staff follow certain rules therefore such as obtaining prior permission from their compliance officer or not trading in any securities that the fund is trading.

Pillar III disclosure Basel II (the banking regulations) requires investment firms to be more transparent by publishing specific details of their risks, and this is referred to as a Pillar III disclosure. Investors should ask to review a copy of the Pillar III disclosure as it is a very good insight into the manager's process of risk assessment.

Prime broker An external service provider that supplies services such as securities lending, leveraged trade executions and cash management, amongst other things to a fund. It is effectively a broker that centralises the portfolio of the fund. When doing so their role is enhanced when the relevant fund needs leverage or to short certain securities as the prime broker will benefit financially from such activities. The prime broker may act as the custodian of the assets therefore. A custodian is a bank that has the right and obligation to hold the financial assets of its clients.

Prospectus A prospectus, also called an offering memorandum or private placement memorandum, is a document that describes the major features of a fund. The prospectus should contain enough detail so that prospective investors may evaluate the fund. For example, a fund's prospectus would outline the risks associated with the fund, the fund's activity, the fund's governing bodies and service providers and the fund's structure. Note however that offshore funds unless they are offered to retail investors are not in any way obligated to include any specific information. Onshore funds on the other hand like UCITS funds in particular are directed to give investors certain information. The prospectus for traditional offshore funds is pretty much written as the manager deems fit, usually on the advice of its lawyers, and not with the idea of protecting investors.

Sharpe ratio The Sharpe ratio measures risk-adjusted performance: it signifies how well the return of an asset compensates the investor for the risk taken. Essentially, it indicates whether a portfolio's returns are a result of smart investment decisions or rather a consequence of excess risk. Although a portfolio or fund can reap higher returns than others, it can only be considered a good investment if such returns are not accompanied by too much additional risk. Portfolios with higher Sharpe ratios have had better risk-adjusted performance.

Side letter A special arrangement which legally binds a fund to giving preferential treatment to some investors over others. Whilst side letters are not uncommon in the fund industry, they are a questionable practice from a corporate governance and ethical point of view. The FSA sets out requirements for managers to disclose the existence of side letters and a failure to disclose is potentially a breach of the FSA's principle that a firm must conduct its business with integrity.

Style drift Style drift occurs where the fund's strategy changes over time. Investors should be wary of managers whose style and approach are uncertain, as usually in difficult markets such managers are more likely to experience difficulties as their performance may become more random.

Ticket Normally within a manager, a trade is done or an order placed which gives rise to a 'ticket.' The trade has to be booked to an account and for various reasons this can sometimes be done after the trade is closed and the result of the trade is known. Regulators and certain industry bodies recommend that the trade or ticket is allocated to an account before the result of the trade is known. This is called a 'pre-allocation of trade' policy. It is not actually compulsory in most jurisdictions, and sometimes the only requirement is that a policy is in place within the manager.

Total expense ratio (TER) The TER is a measure of the total costs associated with managing and operating a fund divided by the fund's total assets. This calculation arrives at a percentage amount that represents the costs to investors as a ration. These costs consist primarily of management fees and additional expenses such as trading fees, legal fees, auditor fees and other operational expenses.

Tracking error/slippage In the context of hedge funds, tracking error refers to the measurement of how much the return on a portfolio deviates from the return on its benchmark index. Slippage often occurs during periods of higher volatility, when market orders are used, and also when large orders are executed when there may not be enough interest at the desired price level to maintain the expected price of trade.

Trade break Trade breaks are un-reconciled positions in the manager's books (accounts). A trade break must be noted and dealt with urgently as it can represent an error from the relevant bank or from the fund, which if unresolved will have financial consequences.

Umbrella fund This is an investment fund that is a single legal entity but that has several sub-funds which are separate and distinct. Each sub-fund will have limited liability status with independent profits and losses. As one legal entity, however, there is only one board and the directors of the umbrella fund have the power to take decisions for each sub-fund. Such umbrella funds can have multiple strategies represented by various sub-funds within the same legal entity.

Undertakings for Collective Investment in Transferable Securities (UCITS) UCITS is a European regulation framework governing the creation and distribution of pooled investment schemes, including mutual funds and exchange-traded funds. A UCITS fund approved by one European state may be moved or 'passported' and distributed to all other member states. Luxembourg, due to the high degree of protection offered to investors, is by far the most popular domicile for UCITS. The Europeans are now on version iv of the UCITS laws and are contemplating version v.

Valuation agent A valuation agent, also known as an administrator, provides valuation services to the fund; that is, it calculates the fund's NAV. *See Administrator.* They may also be used in addition to the administrator as a specialist accountant to price hard to value assets.

Value at risk (VaR) VaR is a risk measure that indicates the risk of loss on a specific portfolio of assets. It is calculated by weighing up the probability of risk (also known as the confidence level) in comparison to the given period of time. VaR is thus a threshold value in which the probability that the predicted market loss on the portfolio over the time period exceeds the (market) value.

Index